PRAYING LIKE JESUS

MW00412743

PRAYING LIKE JESUS

HOWARD W. ROBERTS

United Church Press
Cleveland, Ohio

United Church Press, Cleveland, Ohio 44115
© 1999 by Howard W. Roberts

Biblical quotations, which have been adapted for inclusivity, are from the New Revised Standard Version of the Bible, © 1989 by the Division of Christian Education of the National Council of the Churches of Christ in the U.S.A., and are used by permission

Published 1999. All rights reserved

Printed in the United States of America on acid-free paper

04 03 02 01 00 99 5 4 3 2 1

Library of Congress Cataloging-in-Publication Data

Roberts, Howard W., 1947–
Praying like Jesus / Howard W. Roberts.
p. cm.
Includes bibliographical references.
ISBN 0-8298-1326-8 (pbk. : alk. paper)
1. Jesus Christ—Prayers. 2. Prayer—Christianity. I. Title.
BV229 .R63 1999
232.9'04—ddc21

98-45513
CIP

CONTENTS

Introduction

This book is a journey exploring Jesus' prayers and what it means to pray like Jesus. I'm glad you have joined me for the trip. I hope by book's end we will be soul mates as a result of our sojourn together.

Frankly, when the idea of praying like Jesus first struck me, I wondered, "Would I like to pray like Jesus?" My immediate reaction was, "Certainly. Wouldn't everybody?" However, as I began to explore some of the things Jesus prayed for and to consider some of the things that happened to Jesus as a result of his communion with God, I wasn't so sure I really wanted to pray like Jesus. A colleague expressed struggle similar to mine: "Thoughts about Jesus have troubled my mind in recent days.... The more I read the ancient texts the more I discover a Man in whose thought-world I am not comfortable."[1]

To pray stirs the question, What is God like? That question has dogged me for years. It is the question of a seeker, one in search of knowing God and being known by God. Is it possible to know what God is like? Well, yes and no. Or more accurately, we can partially know what God is like. It is partial knowledge because we who are finite cannot possibly comprehend One who is infinite. We who are temporal cannot grasp One who is eternal. Thus, our question exceeds our answer, our search exceeds our discovery, but question and search we must.

What does it mean to be human? This question also has dogged me. It is related to the first. Actually, to probe one of these questions inevitably means I also will probe the other. Apparently, the earliest biblical storytellers wrestled with the same questions. They said that human beings were created in the image of God. Underneath that statement are my two questions, What is God like, and what does it mean to be human?

My questioning search and probing exploration have led me to the Bible—more specifically, to the Gospels in the Christian Scriptures. Through the Gospels I have begun to formulate a composite portrait of Jesus. Through this portrait I have gained insight into what God is like and what it means to be human.

Recently, what has been most helpful to me has been to explore what, when, where, how, and why Jesus prayed. I think there are clues for us about what God is like and what it means to be human in the prayers of Jesus. What does it mean to pray like Jesus? My quest has informed my questions and helped me to grow in wisdom and in stature with God and people.

In *Praying Like Jesus,* I examine the Gospels and focus on prayers of Jesus as well as times when he prayed. Since prayers are more than words, I examine Jesus' baptism and his wilderness temptation experiences as prayers. Praying like Jesus will lead us to pray for ourselves, friends and enemies, grieving people, worship, and the world. In chapters 8 through 12, I have included prayers I have written to illustrate what I am suggesting.

My tendency is to express things chronologically. However, seldom is there any situation or event in our lives that we ever follow from its inception, except perhaps the lives of our children. For all other events we come in somewhere in the middle of things and seek to piece together the order in which things happened that took a particular direction or evolved to the point where it is now. Although the Gospels seek to give some chronological order to the life of Jesus based on the authors' purposes and intentions, the story was not put together chronologically. It was pieced together backward. Supporting evidence is the disproportionate amount of material that deals with the last week of Jesus' life and the minute amount given to the beginning of his life. Only two of the Gospels have anything about Jesus' birth. All four Gospels have extensive information about Jesus' last week, his death, burial, and resurrection. Apparently, from the beginning of telling the good news, it was told backward from Easter.

I examine praying like Jesus in much the same manner. I begin with Jesus' prayer in the Garden of Gethsemane. I have discovered that people die the way they live. By learning how to die, people learn how to live. Jesus' agony in Gethsemane as he faced death clearly indicates how he approached life. The prayer of Jesus recorded as occurring in Gethsemane is the genuine Lord's Prayer. Exploration of this prayer at the outset will guide, shape, and influence my understanding of what it means to pray like Jesus.

What is clear in Jesus' prayer in Gethsemane about his approach to life and death will be seen as glimpses and hints in his other prayers that we investigate. The result will be not only an exploration of Jesus' prayers but also insight into what it means to pray like Jesus.

The following pages of this book describe the result of my journey to this point of what it means to pray like Jesus. What you read here is by no means conclusive or exhaustive but a continuation of my examination and exploration of, and my struggle with, what God is like, what it means to be human, and what it means to pray like Jesus. May the words you read contribute to your probing and searching what God is like, what it means for you to be human, and what praying like Jesus involves for you. May the words you read encourage and challenge you to be more fully human. May the result be that you have a better understanding of what God is like and what it means to be created in the image of God. May *Praying Like Jesus* contribute to your being what God created you to be, the best human being you can be. As you pray like Jesus, may your faith be deepened, your hope heightened, your vision broadened, and may you grow in wisdom and stature with God and people.

CHAPTER ONE

Jesus Agonized

MARK 14:32–42

Any intimate relationship requires a tremendous amount of time and energy for communication. The more intimate a relationship is, the greater the need for communication between the people involved. Intimate friendships require much communication. If the communication level does not deepen, the relationship does not deepen. To know and to be known require self-revelation. Self-revelation involves trust, openness, confidence, and confidentiality. These characteristics contribute to intimate bonding.

The stories we have about Jesus disclose there was an intimate bonding between Jesus and God. Examining the Gospels in an effort to gain a clearer understanding of who Jesus was and what his relationship with God was like, I have discovered Jesus' communion with God intensified as he moved closer and closer to the last days of his life. The strongest evidence of intimate bonding with God is demonstrated in Jesus' prayer in the Garden of Gethsemane. There is no positive way to know how the Gospel writers collected the words of Jesus' Gethsemane prayer. I assume that Jesus told Peter, James, and John what he prayed because he left them a stone's throw away when he went on to pray. Maybe they overheard Jesus' prayer, but surely hearing such a prayer would have heightened their consciousness rather than drugged them into sleep. Regardless of how the content of the prayer came to be known, Matthew, Mark, and Luke gave accounts of it. In some manuscripts Luke added a phrase about Jesus sweating "like drops of blood." Maybe that was Luke's way of capturing verbally the agony of Jesus that had been described to him or the agony that he projected as he thought about this prayer experience of Jesus.

Sweating was a significant part of Jesus' praying in Gethsemane. Sweating is a distinctly human function. Sweating indicates the temperature is hot or our bodies have had a strenuous workout. If a task is not difficult, we may comment, "No sweat." If someone is concerned about an impending situation, we may advise, "Don't sweat it." Sweating is a sign our bodies are responding to temperature, work, exertion, and pressure. We could learn a lot about ourselves by examining what makes us sweat.

What makes you sweat? Does physical labor or exercise? Do you ever break out in a "cold sweat"? Do you sweat when you are tense? When you struggle and agonize about a situation in your life, do you sweat?

Jesus was a distinct human being who sweated. Luke wrote that Jesus' sweat resulted from an agonizing inner struggle. His sweat was "like great drops of blood falling down on the ground" (Luke 22:44—many manuscripts do not have verses 43–44). That is some sweat! Anything that made Jesus sweat like that has to be examined.

I wish you could visit Gethsemane. I especially wish you could be there at night and get a sense of the sounds, sights, smells, and darkness that engulf the place. Although city surrounds it now and no one is encouraged to go there at night, a night visit is moving. In Jesus' time a night visit was frightening because it was far from the city, through the Kidron Valley, in the desert, and the fears of evil were lurking there. That was why so many Roman soldiers went with Judas. They did not want to go there alone.

The intimacy Jesus felt with God is captured in his simple, repetitive prayer: "Abba, for you all things are possible; remove this cup from me; yet, not what I want, but what you want" (Mark 14:36). So much is packed in so few words. That's how intimacy is. Each word carries a potent message. As we unpack this prayer, we gain insight and understanding into Jesus' relationship with God.

In his account, Mark retained the native Aramaic word *Abba* that Jesus used to address God. The word itself conveys intimacy. *Abba* is warm, close, and personal like our word "Daddy."[1] While living with an Israeli family, repeatedly I heard the fourteen-year-old girl address her dad with the word *Abba.* Will Campbell has observed, "Abba sounded like some kind of baby talk to one's daddy. Or the way we talk to little babies when we are pretending they are talking to us. . . . Abba. Daddy. Pop. Pater Noster. Vater Unser. Uren Fader. Notre Pere. Nostro Papa."[2]

I wonder what Jesus meant when he said to God, "For you all things are possible"? Evidently, one of the things it meant—or Jesus wanted it to mean—was to get him out of there. It took no genius to read the current climate and events and know that Jesus' time was limited. He knew that continuing his ministry as he had been doing would be the end for him.

Was it possible for God to swoop in and snatch Jesus away in the darkness of the night? It was not possible without breaking the natural laws with which every other human being must cope. What would that say about Jesus? Would that suggest that he had a special arrangement with God and that when things got too tough, God would rescue him?

What did Jesus mean by that statement, "Abba, for you all things are possible"? One possibility was to escape. He could slip away in the night and never be heard from again. Surely, he considered that. Wouldn't you? That was an option for Jesus, and he showed on numerous occasions that he considered the options before choosing one.

Another option was to cut a deal with the authorities. He could have gone to the authorities and admitted that he had created quite a stir around there and that he was willing to tone down his rhetoric or even shut up completely. Then they would not have to worry about him anymore. The authorities might have been uncomfortable with that, but it would have made life a lot easier for them. Surely, those thoughts ran through Jesus' mind as he felt the pressure, struggled with the feeling of having no outlet, wondered what he was going to do, and voiced to God, "For you all things are possible."

If anyone ever said to God, "Get me out of this mess," Jesus said it. His words were, "Remove this cup [of suffering] from me." Three times he prayed the same thing. Jesus was not repeating his prayer for effect. The repetition was not an indication of begging; rather, it was evidence of agony. The repetition demonstrated that Jesus felt the pressure and was wrestling with the temptation to seek safety and security. But he did not give in to the pressure. He perceived the temptation to seek safety and security as blindness, and he came to restore sight, not to diminish it. In spite of the obstructor posting the sign "No Outlet," Jesus knew there were ways out, and God was the Source of hope and help to find the way.

If we want to identify a prayer as the Lord's Prayer, I nominate this one. What popularly is known as the Lord's Prayer would be more appropriately identified as the Learner's Prayer, and these agonizing words formed into a prayer in Gethsemane would be the Lord's Prayer. This prayer is personal, intimate, intense, and expressive of Jesus' struggle and need.

Notice the commanding, demanding expression in the statement "Remove this cup from me." Was that any way to talk to God? It certainly was! Jesus had developed an intimate relationship with God. One of the merits of intimacy is that it causes people to be open to each other. Jesus had the kind of relationship with God that allowed, even demanded, that he express exactly what he thought, how he felt, and what he wondered.

Jesus' wanting the cup of suffering removed was an expression of ambiguity. He wanted the suffering removed, and he wanted to do God's will. Therein lay the tension and struggle that created agony for Jesus and thus his ambiguity. We want absolutes. We want magic formulas that make everything work out the right way, neatly and simply. Gethsemane was not a place of magic. It was a place of agony. There we see faith in action, the kind of faith that brings out sweat, blood, and tears.

Jesus wanted two things: the cup of suffering to pass from him and God's will to be done. Jesus was under pressure because the two things were in conflict. The conflict created agony for Jesus. There seemed to be no way out.

Rather than understanding prayer as communion with God, we have viewed prayer as an attempt to bend the will of God. This approach has been built on the assumption that human will and God's will always are in conflict. When prayer is based on this assumption, the only way out is to baptize the outcome with the phrase "Not my will but yours be done." Then whatever happens is interpreted as God's will. Many people have died of disease, and family members have concluded, "It was God's will." What about the medical team that worked so hard on the side of health and wholeness? Were they working against God's will? If they were, then why is God so cruel as to have people expend the best they have for nothing?

The phrase "Yet, not what I want, but what you want," spoken forcefully by Jesus, has become an expression of sad resignation when spoken by persons who then identify whatever happens as God's will. In this way, people have blamed God for many unjust acts, including murder, extortion, and prejudice. Mark made the point that the phrase was neither sad resignation nor submission for Jesus by recording that Jesus prayed the same prayer three times. Jesus was not approaching his situation in an effort to bend the will of God as if his will and God's will were in conflict. After considering all the possibilities and making his appeal that his life not end then, Jesus could say, "Not what I want, but what you want." Then Jesus was free to accept or reject God's response. The utterance "what you want" was voluntary rather than the result of a trap that God had set in which Jesus was caught. Jesus' prayer indicated his need to say what he wanted and the importance of saying no to some things before feeling freed to say yes.

It was not God's will that Jesus be executed like a common criminal. That was the will of the people. Jesus' prayer in the Garden of Gethsemane is a key to understanding prayer as communication. We need to consider prayer from the position of communication rather than will. This is really Jesus' prayer with regard to his personal anguish and need. God's will was for Jesus to be faithful in communicating and conveying God's love for the world. The more faithful Jesus was in loving the world, the more the world resisted this love and the One who embodied it. Jesus' love for the world and the world's resistance to this love created such tension and pressure and conflict that Jesus' sweat was "like drops of blood."

We get clues about how Jesus lived as we examine how he faced death. Learning how to die is a prerequisite for learning how to live. A German mystic observed, "Who dies not before he dies is ruined when he dies."[3] Only in facing our limitations, of which mortality is the big one, are we able really to know how to live. The secret to Jesus' life is disclosed in his prayer in Gethsemane.

Jesus' closeness to God did not mean he had less need for prayer; it meant he had more need for prayer. If we are serious about praying like Jesus, we will discover that we need a close, intimate relationship with God. The closer and more intimate we become with God, the greater is our need to commune with God. Prayer is the communication system between people and God. The more abstract and detached a relationship is, the less need there is for communication. Such is true of a person's relationship with God. The more intimate the relationship, the more involved (not more complicated or complex but more involved) the communication process needs to be.

For Jesus, the more intimate his relationship with God became, the more treacherous and precarious life became. At a superficial level, there is a sense in which life would have been easier, simpler, and less stressful if Jesus had kept his distance from God. The more intensely involved Jesus became with God, the more intense and costly were the decisions he had to make. When it was time for serious decision making, the more costly those decisions seemed to be for Jesus, and yet the clearer Jesus seemed to be about the decisions he made.

Jesus' relationship with God was clear and costly. Praying like Jesus presupposes an intimate relationship with God. Praying like Jesus can be as clarifying and costly for us as it was for Jesus. Why should we expect life to be less costly for us than it was for him?

Have you ever thought as I have? There have been times in my life when I thought of prayer as a special, magical formula, although I would not have used the word "magical." My view was that if I said a prayer in the right way at the right time for the right reason, I would be protected from hardships, struggles, disappointments, and tragedies. The safe loophole in this line of thinking was that if I were not protected, then I had not said the prayer in the right way or for the right reason or at the right time. Gillian Leslie has noted, "The comfort of prayer lies, not in an almost magical ability to smooth our troubles away, but in its power to strengthen us to meet the troubles that must inevitably come."[4] This explains why prayer always has been more popular in theory than in practice.

I have yet to meet the person who journeyed from womb to tomb without coming up against some events and experiences that slowed her down, altered her course, and kept her from taking the most direct route through life. You and I have been cruising through life when suddenly we were hit broadside with a disease, the loss of a job, the need for surgery, the death of a family member, a war that broke out, a federal building that was bombed, or a tornado that ripped through the community. There was no way emotionally that we could continue straight ahead on the route we were taking. We were slammed into an emotional detour. We felt that there was no way out. However, as we wrestled and struggled with the impact of the crisis, we found ourselves exploring and taking alternate routes that required more time and energy to get us to our destinations. In hindsight, we observe that it would have been impossible to have done anything other than take alternate routes. It really was and is true that there are situations where the only way out is the way through, but the way through is not always the most direct route—although often it is the more scenic one. Usually, these situations are frustrating, painful, and disruptive, but they may be the times when we learn the most about ourselves and gain clarity about the meaning and purpose of our lives.

The most agonizing prayer Jesus prayed was in Gethsemane. What we are told about Jesus through that prayer is that prayer was the culmination of Jesus' praying his life. The agonizing expressions of Jesus to God in his prayer in Gethsemane were the result of his praying all along the journey of his life. The Gethsemane prayer was not a last-ditch, desperate attempt to get God to listen to him or to get God on his side. The prayer was an expression of the truth that the way out is the way through.

I've learned the most about hope and how it keeps life alive by examining the life of Jesus. In his life, hope provided the energy that constantly replenished and motivated his will. There were numerous times in Jesus' life when someone threw up a roadblock with the words "No Outlet" written boldly across it. There was forever someone—Pharisee, Sadducee, a disciple here, or a tax collector there—holding up a sign in front of Jesus that said, "No Outlet." At the outset of Jesus' ministry following his first sermon in the Nazareth synagogue, the people became so upset with Jesus' application of Scripture that they closed in on him and were ready to kill him. What a way to start in the ministry! It was a preview of coming distractions.

Repeatedly, Jesus was squeezed in by his actions and the responses of people, especially members of the religious establishment. People intentionally tried to trap Jesus. Regardless of the form the trap took, the sign always was the same: "No Outlet."

To see a "No Outlet" sign along the highway triggers a mental debate for me. I argue, "That isn't true. I'll bet there is a way out." In fact there is. The worst scenario is that I can backtrack from a place and get out. I've gotten myself into some tight spots verbally and gotten the message loud and clear that there was no way out other than to backpedal or lose face, admit my mistake, and leave. These are ways out, and they disprove the sign "No Outlet." But Jesus refused to be trapped by either/or situations. He was able to perceive a third alternative to the routes that appeared to have no outlet.

Just before the end of Jesus' life is the most distinct "no outlet" situation he experienced. Jesus and his disciples left their Passover meal and went to the Mount of Olives. It is just across the Kidron Valley from Jerusalem. The Garden of Gethsemane is near the base of the Mount of Olives. A grove of gnarled old olive trees can be seen there; at least one of them is nearly fifteen hundred years old. The name *Gethsemane* means "wine press" or "oil press." It was an appropriate place for one to struggle under pressure, wrestle with the sign "No Outlet," and sweat out a decision. What a graphic portrayal of prayer, of what it means to pray like Jesus.

Jesus was in intense agony in Gethsemane. There he struggled with life and death, success and failure, friends and foes, pain and pleasure, suffering and redemption. There, as never before, Jesus was tempted to seek safety. He felt the pressure. One sign of the pressure was that, according to Matthew and Mark, Jesus threw himself face-down on the ground. The position of prayer for Jews was either standing or lying straight out on the ground. Prostration most often was the prayer position of one intensely agonizing about something in communion with God. Jesus felt the pressure squeezing him.

People reveal a lot about themselves by their reactions to pressure. In Gethsemane, Jesus' personality and character were laid bare. He knew that a direct confrontation was at hand, and he wanted to avoid it if possible. But Jesus also knew that the source of healing for his life, for all lives, is in mourning the losses the world inflicts. Jesus knew that the source of cruelty lies in the rejection of our suffering. As Henri Nouwen observed, "Those who try to avoid having their hearts broken end up in hell."[5]

In his desire to understand and be prepared to face the complexities ahead of him, Jesus went to Gethsemane to pray. He invited Peter, James, and John to go with him. He asked them to watch and pray while he went on a little farther to be alone with the Alone. Are there some times when we want to be alone with God, but we want some loyal supporters nearby? At times when we are asked to be the loyal supporters, the agony and struggle that another experiences are more than we seem capable or willing to face. We find ways to deny what is happening.

Denial is a common coping mechanism that we use to avoid facing and dealing with painful issues and events. One common method of denial is to sleep. A depressed person does not or cannot face reality and thus seeks to withdraw from life. Sleep is one method of withdrawal. In the Garden of Gethsemane is a blatant example of the disciples using denial to cope with the stress and pressure they felt.

Jesus needed his disciples to watch with him. He especially needed the support of those who had been closest to him. He wanted and needed them to bear his burden with him. But what happened?

While he went on farther to pray in solitude, Peter, James, and John went to sleep. Three times Jesus expressed his struggle and agony to the three disciples and solicited their help and support. And each time, the disciples responded the same way. They went to sleep. How upsetting, how disappointing, that must have been! When Jesus returned to them, he sought to respond to their denial by asking them if they could not stay awake for one hour. He urged them to watch and pray so they might not enter into temptation. Jesus was preparing himself for what he sensed was coming. He sought to get his disciples to prepare themselves, but it was too painful for them. They preferred to avoid the painful thoughts of what might happen, so they went to sleep. It was the perfect, passive form of denial.

I wonder what would have happened had Peter and the others remained awake, watched, and prayed. Would they have been better prepared to face the events that transpired? Would Peter have been less eager to resort to violence at the time of the arrest? Would Peter have been more willing to stand up for Jesus in the courtyard of the high priest? Would they have seen the sign "No Outlet" as untrue?

As painful and burdensome as life was becoming for Jesus, he sought to prepare himself in communion with God. In the face of the burden and pain that Peter, James, and John sensed that Jesus was experiencing, they went to sleep. It was more than they were willing to face. Sleeping was the easiest way they knew to deny what was happening. They preferred to cope that way rather than to watch and pray. When the worst came only hours later, Peter, James, and John were unprepared to deal with it, and Peter's denial, and perhaps that of James and John, became aggressive, even more blatant than their sleeping in Gethsemane. When Jesus needed the support and care of the people closest to him, they were asleep. Their sleeping in Gethsemane was a strong hint of the lack of support Jesus would receive from his disciples in the hours to come.

Later that evening while they were in the Garden of Gethsemane, the soldiers came to arrest Jesus. Once again Peter sought to be the obstructor. He attempted to deny what was taking place by using violence to keep violence from happening. He jerked out his sword and took off Malchus's ear. I don't know if that was a warning blow of what was to come or if Peter was just so off the mark with his sword as he had been so often with his statements. Jesus responded to the denial by telling Peter to put the sword away and to quit getting in the way of his being the Messiah, the Child of the living God.

In the Garden of Gethsemane Jesus climbed the stony, mountain path of agony. He struggled with the anxiety that events of his life were causing. He struggled with the disappointment that his disciples seemed unable to comprehend his ministry. Even in the midst of his most agonizing prayer, his disappointment was intensified because the three disciples who had come with him could not agonize with him and fell asleep. He suffered nearly as much from his friends as he did from his enemies. Maybe all of that made the writer of Hebrews conclude that Jesus made his prayers and requests with loud cries and tears to God (Heb. 5:7). Of all the agonizing struggles Jesus experienced, of all the mountain paths Jesus climbed, the one in Gethsemane was the toughest. Climbing that mountain of agony made him sweat "like drops of blood."

Christ did not agonize in Gethsemane so that we could have a warm feeling inside. The agony for Jesus, the sacrifice he made, was in being faithful to God. His struggle demands that we struggle. The struggle and sacrifice we are to make are to be faithful to God. Each of us has been given the gift of living one life and dying one death. There is no escape, no outlet from this. When the time comes for us to walk our lonesome valleys, let us take heart in the fact that we do not have to walk them by ourselves. The life-giving Sovereign is there to join us in the journey up the mountain road of agony, through the gardens and the valleys, to sweat along with us, and to support us as we face our "No Outlets," encouraging us to be faithful to God.

The only place in Jesus' life, the only place in our lives, where "No Outlet" is undisputed is death. It is true that we cannot and will not get out of this life alive. We can't backpedal on this one. Regardless of how confident our faith in God makes us, in spite of how assured we may be of resurrection, even though we may see the exit from this life as entrance into another life, there is no outlet from facing death.

Maybe it is only when we come to terms with our own deaths that we ever pray like Jesus.

Jesus refused to be trapped by people or circumstances. He debated, resisted, and found alternatives to all the "No Outlet" signs that people and circumstances constructed along his journey. And when his life ran headlong into the one event, death, from which there truly was no outlet, he faced that situation openly, prayerfully, and honestly with God, assured that with God all things were possible including confronting the one "No Outlet" that life held for him and for all who are created in the image of God.

QUESTIONS TO PONDER

1. Why do you think Jesus' praying in the Garden of Gethsemane was agonizing?
2. Jesus said in his prayer that with God all things are possible. Name at least four things you think were possible for God in this situation.
3. What event or events have caused prayer to be an agonizing experience for you?
4. What things were possible for God in your situation?
5. What is God's will?
6. Was it God's will that Jesus die? What kind of portrait of God does your answer paint?
7. Do you think that God's will is going to be done no matter what we do? What impact does what we do have on God's will? What impact does God's will have on what we do?

CHAPTER TWO

Jesus Prayed His Life

LUKE 22:7–30

In exploring the theme of praying like Jesus, I am going backward. In chapter 1, I invited you to explore with me a prayer Jesus prayed the last night of his life. Now, consider with me the entire episode of the last Passover meal Jesus shared with his disciples as a prayer. I'm convinced that "words and activities only get us underway in prayer. Prayer itself represents the deepest, most heartfelt, most agonizing concerns of our inner selves."[1]

If you want to know what a person thinks about God, pay attention to that person's prayers. If carried to their logical conclusion, what does God look like through the eyes of the person's prayers? Exploring Jesus' prayers is an excellent way to get a clear impression of what God was like and who God was to Jesus.

By the time anyone got around to writing anything down about the life and ministry of Jesus, twenty-five years had passed since his death and resurrection. In some letters to early churches, Paul was the first to put anything on papyrus. That was late in the 50s, 57 or 58 C.E. Matthew, Mark, and Luke wrote in the 60s. The intended effort of these four writers was to announce a message, not to write history. They began with the resurrection and worked backward in collecting their information. Then when they wrote, the resurrection was their focus and where they were headed with their narratives. As a result, we have a disproportionate amount of material related to the last week of Jesus' life and, in comparison, almost nothing from Jesus' childhood and very little from his ministry.

The evidence is irrefutable that Jesus laid out a life the way a life devoted to God is to be laid out. In this sense, we could conclude that all of his life was a prayer to God. Glenn Hinson has noted, "If only we knew how to look at life as God sees it, all of life could become a prayer."[2] Ken Medema, a composer, stated it this way: "My prayer life is more exciting than ever. I don't do a lot of the 'out loud' praying, but rather, prayer is like breathing. I am aware every hour of every day that I am taking my life experience and taking my world to God, asking for direction and guidance. I often just make comments to God about what I'm seeing, hearing, and feeling. It's sort of like an ongoing conversation."[3] More than anyone, Jesus knew how to look at life as God sees it. As a result of seeing life as God sees it, Jesus' life became a prayer.

In this sense, the scriptural passage (Luke 22:7–30) describes a part of Jesus' life as a prayer set in the context of the last meal Jesus shared with his disciples. The central event that comes out of this text for Christians is the institution of communion, or the eucharist. However, it is important to explore what precedes and what follows the central event in the text. Luke set the meal in the context of Passover. The Passover lamb was a seal of the covenant, and the Passover meal commemorated the covenant offered to the faith community by the God who sets people free.

In a consideration of this Passover meal as an illustration of Jesus praying his life, several things are helpful. First, note the symbolism and meaning of the elements of the meal. Second, consider the purpose and intent of the meal. Third, look at the people present at the meal. Fourth, all of these aspects combine to make this Passover experience a prayer of Jesus that becomes the closing parenthesis on praying his life.

Prominent rabbis often kept the Passover with their disciples. Thus, Jesus met with his disciples. It is unclear whether all of his disciples gathered with him for the Passover. Certainly, the twelve apostles were there. The disciples had gotten things ready for the meal in a prearranged location. At the appointed time, Jesus joined them for the meal. Someone has suggested that Leonardo da Vinci's painting *The Last Supper* has influenced some translators of Luke's account of the Last Supper when they translated, "He sat at table" (22:14 RSV). In those days people did not sit at a table. They reclined alongside a table.

Usually at the Passover meal, each person had a cup, and the cup was filled four times because four cups of wine were to be consumed. The meal began with everyone drinking a cup of wine. Jesus took his cup and gave thanks to God. His giving thanks probably was the traditional Jewish benediction pronounced over the bread and wine.

Blessed art Thou, O Lord our God, King of the Universe,
who bringest forth bread from the earth.
Blessed art Thou, O Lord our God, King of the Universe,
who createst the fruit of the vine.[4]

God is the One blessed and not the wine or the bread.

Giving thanks like that was customary of Jesus. He always received what was given to him as a gift. He gave thanks for the gift. Then he gave the gift away. At the supper he invited his disciples to share the gift as he gave the gift away to them. That was the way he had understood his life. He had received his life as a gift from God. He gave thanks for the gift, and he gave his life away in love, acting out the love and grace of God for all people.

At the Passover meal following the first cup of wine, each participant dipped a vegetable into salt water as a way of recalling the crossing of the sea to escape from slavery. Luke did not give us every detail of the meal, but we can assume that Jesus dipped a vegetable into the salt water not only to recall the escape from slavery by his ancestors but also to call attention to the deliverance from oppression, hatred, denial, and betrayal that had been his ministry and to which he was inviting disciples to join and carry out in his absence. Then a piece of matzo, unleavened bread, was eaten, recalling the haste with which the Israelites fled Egypt. Jesus took a piece of bread and broke it. He urged them to remember him. He suggested that whenever they got together and shared a meal, their collective memory could turn a regular, ordinary meal into a sacred experience as they remembered him. This was an acknowledgment that when people gather together and share a meal, the whole is more than the sum of the people present, and that is increased exponentially by collectively remembering one who has been with them but is no longer present. To remember Jesus meant to remember who he was to them, what they had shared together, what he sought to accomplish through his ministry with them, and how they were continuing what Jesus had set out to do. Perhaps Jesus was praying that they be in haste to set people free from whatever imprisoned or oppressed them. The breaking of a piece of bread was Jesus praying for the brokenness that he and they must experience caused by the losses the world inflicted on them. A failure to experience and mourn the losses meant healing and wholeness could not occur. As his ancestors had to mourn their losses in leaving Egypt in order to be healed, so he and his disciples had to mourn the losses the world was inflicting on them.

At first Jesus' ancestors were just relieved to escape Egypt. However, after some time to reflect in the context of a difficult, weary desert wilderness journey, they began to remember the "good old days" in Egypt, which had not been as good as they remembered. When they failed or refused to mourn their losses, they became a group of whiners and complainers. For some reason it was only after the death of Moses that they seemed able and willing to mourn their losses. Once they did that, they were then shaped into a new people. Jesus was praying that his life and ministry, along with those of his disciples, might help people in a new generation and in every generation to mourn their losses inflicted by the world so that God could give them new lives and shape them into a new people.

After the main course of lamb, the second cup of wine was drunk. It was the most important cup of the four. At that time the person narrated the Exodus story. There was a double orientation of the second cup. It looked back gratefully to God's past saving act and eagerly anticipated the future redemption. The blood of the Passover lambs had been a sign of salvation at the beginning of Israel's history.

Luke highlighted the second cup in his account of the meal. Jesus called attention to the covenant concept that was part of the Passover-Exodus experience. In his forward looking from the vantage of this Passover Jesus called out to his disciples to move toward and into a New Covenant. It was a continuation and recasting of the old. The theme was the same—deliverance, liberation, salvation. The life of the Passover lambs was in their blood. Jesus described his own life in similar language. Pouring out his life was like pouring out his blood. Jesus willingly poured out his life in love, demonstrating the extent to which he was willing to go to communicate what it means to be loved by God. Perhaps only when we are able and willing to go that far in love are we truly being the redeeming people of God.

The Passover meal, though linked to a historical event, was a forward-looking meal. It was forward looking because the food at the first Passover was eaten after the family had packed their bags for the journey to the promised land. As Jesus shared his last Passover with his disciples, everything in the account suggests that Jesus was looking forward, not backward.

The Passover meal was shared with at least ten people. Do you know why the number ten was used? The average lamb would provide enough food for ten people. On the surface of things, we don't know much about the dietary rules mentioned in the Hebrew Scriptures. However, exploration of those rules usually reveals some quite practical reasons for the regulations. That's true of the number of people who were to share the Passover meal.

Jesus took the cup and the bread and gave a radical reinterpretation of the meal. He was pointing to a new exodus. In the old exodus the people had been set free from slavery to the Egyptians. In the new exodus people would be set free from slavery to sin.

Although each person had his own cup, Jesus gave his cup to his disciples and instructed them, "Take this and divide it among yourselves." The Passover lamb was not a sin offering but a seal of a covenant with God. The cup signified a New Covenant being offered to the faith community by the God who sets people free. Those who drank from the cup were entering into a covenant that offered a new kind of freedom, a release from captivity to sin and death, a New Covenant extended by a liberating God to all who believe, Jew and Gentile. Those who share in this covenant are joined to one another, life to life, as signified and sealed in the cup shared among themselves.

By drinking from the cup and eating from the loaf, they signified receiving the gift of liberation and their promise to be partners with Christ in the ministry of liberation. To drink from Jesus' cup revealed a unity of fellowship and a sharing in the sufferings of Jesus. It was to say they were committed to the same type of ministry with the similar risks and threats as Jesus' ministry had involved. To partake of the one loaf was an expression of the oneness of the new community created by redemptive self-giving love. And to eat from the loaf was a commitment to live in a lovingly redemptive, self-giving way toward others.

In the typical organization of human society, the person who sits at the table is considered superior to the person who serves the table. Jesus reversed that by instituting a revolutionary approach to relationships: the greatest person is the one who serves others. He invited people to join the revolution symbolized by drinking from the cup and eating from the loaf. That was a powerful prayer of promise for Jesus, and it was an invitation to the disciples to join him in praying their lives in the same way he had prayed his.

Of the five places in the Christian Scriptures that tell about this meal (Matt. 26:26–30; Mark 14:22–26; Luke 22:14–30; John 13:1–30; 1 Cor. 11:23–25), leave it to Luke to tell it differently. Luke seems to have combined two traditions about the meal. One had to do with Passover, and the other with sacrifice and the use of sacrificial language. Although many later interpreted the meal to represent the atonement for sin, that was not Luke's intent. Clearly, he tied the meal and its meaning to the Passover, which was a liberation celebration, not an atonement experience.

Luke had Judas participating in the meal, drinking from the cup, and eating from the loaf. Jesus stated that the one who would betray him was at the table with him. Matthew and Mark were not so clear or specific, and according to them, one could argue that Judas was absent at the time of the meal now referred to as the Last Supper.

When Jesus said that the one who would betray him was at the table with him, the disciples reacted by asking, "Surely not I?" (Matt. 26:22). The phrasing expected the negative reply. Judas was the one who did the overt act, yet there was a sense in which all of the disciples betrayed Jesus.

Luke presented the argument among the disciples about who would be the greatest in the realm of God taking place at the last meal they shared with Jesus. The implication as Luke told the story is that all of the Twelve were involved in the argument. Other Gospel writers had the greatness argument taking place another time and involving only James and John. Maybe they argued more than once about greatness. Maybe all of them got into the debate the last night they spent with Jesus. There is something realistic about that. When the foreboding sense of a final farewell hovers over people, there is an urge to get everything in order and often to seek what will make them secure. There also is something terribly selfish, self-serving, and superficial about such a concern.

The way Luke told it makes the event relevant and contemporary. Luke spoke strong words to the church, the church in the first century and the church in the twenty-first century. He said that betrayal had occurred, and it can occur again among those who partake of Holy Communion. And it has, hasn't it? Is there anyone who has partaken of Holy Communion who has not betrayed Christ? Luke said that the greatness dispute at the table in the first century is a real possibility for those in any century who share the cup and loaf. The love of place and power was a problem for the first followers of Christ. We postmodern followers are no different.

We have four Gospels in the Christian Scriptures, and all are about the life and ministry of Jesus. All have information that is common to the others. Each has some information unique to each writer. The order of events varies between the writers because they weren't writing history. They were announcing a message. The intent of the message and the audience to which it was directed had an impact on how the writer announced the message. So Luke told it differently from Matthew, Mark, and John.

We define prayer too narrowly. Our image of prayer is heads bowed, hands folded, and eyes closed. Seldom do we consider an action or an activity as prayer. I do my best praying while I swim. I am able to free-associate with God as I'm exercising my body. Swimming requires me to keep my mouth shut. I listen better. This activity provides an excellent opportunity for me to order my day, examine what I need to do, and offer the day and all that I do with this gift of another day to God. Therefore, everything I do during the day is part of my communion with God. Brother Lawrence had a similar approach as he worked in the kitchen of the monastery. He called it practicing the presence of God. Mother Teresa had this approach toward her work in Calcutta. Glenn Hinson has this experience through his daily walks to and from work. Others have similar experiences as they jog or run. The source for this approach is the life of Jesus. Certainly, there were times when Jesus wanted and needed to express his communion with God in words. That was evident as I noted in the previous chapter. Of course, there were times when Jesus needed to retreat from the demands of interaction with people in order to focus on his relationship with God. All of those efforts—words, retreats, engaging with others—were threads in the tapestry of Jesus praying his life. We can see that most clearly culminated and summarized in the last Passover meal Jesus ate with his disciples.

As Luke told differently how the Last Supper took place and tied it specifically to Passover, there is a strong sense that the whole event was a prayer offered to God by Jesus. The event was a microcosm of what Jesus had done throughout his ministry. He had been praying his life, and he invited his followers to do the same.

By praying his life, Jesus did some strange things. A couple of them are evident at Jesus' last meal. What kind of person was Jesus, who would allow the person who betrayed him and those who argued about being the greatest in God's realm to be at the table with him? Eating together implied friendship and a renunciation of hostile intentions. Why would Jesus let them eat with him? Why would he let them drink from the cup and eat from the loaf?

I have often experienced conversations that I identified as prayers. The other person and I did not bow our heads. Yet the intent, the purpose, the direction of our conversation was of such a nature that God was an intimate part of the conversation and the entire time we were communing with God. That must have been what Jesus meant when he said that where two or three are gathered together for the purpose of engaging God in their lives, indeed God is in their midst. That was the backdrop of the Passover meal. It was a time to share a meal and remember God's presence during the meal, guidance from the meal through the desert, and deliverance from slavery into relationship. The promised land was not nearly so important as a piece of geography as it was a relationship, a relationship between people and God.

Thus, Jesus could share a meal with his disciples and talk about relationship, a new relationship—new in the sense that they hadn't gotten the point yet. It was new in the sense that it was what Jesus had been talking about all along. Perhaps if they heard it again in the context of an important, familiar meal, they would hear the message loud and clear, new, as if for the first time, although the message of liberation was as old as God and as new as the latest person who experiences this amazing grace-filled relationship.

If this Passover meal serves as a microcosm of Jesus praying his life, what might the content of such a prayer be? For what was Jesus praying as he shared the meal with his disciples? A cacophony of sights, sounds, smells, tastes, and feelings are associated with the Passover meal. They were a part of Jesus' experience, and they disclose to us how the last meal Jesus shared with his disciples was a prayer that summarized Jesus praying his life. Let's consider the senses that Jesus might have had during the meal. Perhaps the more senses we sense, the more sense this event will make in Jesus' life.

The Passover meal represented everything Jesus wanted to do with his life. It signified for him what it meant to be in communion with God. It was the heritage in which his life was rooted. God has always been on the side of oppressed people. Throughout his life,

Jesus had a growing understanding of and compassion for oppressed and outcast people. In his ministry Jesus sided with outcasts and sought to be a conveyer of God's deliverance to them. This deliverance motif was present at the table as Jesus shared Passover with his disciples. Look at who was there and what they represented. There were people who wanted power, fame, and recognition. Jesus offered his life, hoping they would see that the road to greatness is paved with service. There were people who would deny any relationship with him and who would betray him. Jesus sought to stay in relationship with them, no matter what they did, in an effort to deliver them, redeem them from the destructiveness of their efforts. His prayer was that all of them would be delivered from doing evil, that none of them would be led into temptation. Goethe is credited with the observation that the highest cannot be spoken; it can only be acted. In this sense the Passover meal was the acting out not only of what God had done but also of what Jesus was seeking to do with his life. Jesus' intent was to live out as fully and completely as he could what it meant to be a servant of God created in the image of God, and it was symbolized in the Passover meal.

What we hear coming from that meal were sadness and sorrow, hurt and bitterness because people had been oppressed, outcast, abused, and treated with malice. All that happened in Egypt to Jesus' ancestors, but it didn't stop there. He had seen it daily during his ministry—a woman caught in adultery, a man forced by the community to live in the cemetery. There also was the sound of noisy laughter as people experienced love and forgiveness and their lives were healed—Bartimaeus could see, a boy with epilepsy was made well. There was warmth like that one feels on a fresh spring day as acceptance was experienced around the Passover meal and as we think about the impact this has on our lives—Judas was still accepted by Jesus and Jesus kept the door of relationship open to him. God is still in the accepting business, healing our brokenness and seeking to help us pick up the pieces and put our lives back together. There was the noisy clanging of chains and the swinging open of iron doors as Jesus visualized captives being set free and the enslaved being released.

Considering who was at the table at Jesus' last meal will be insightful about who is welcome at the table today. They were ordinary people who made an extraordinary mixture.

Matthew was a tax collector. Many regarded him as a man who sold himself into the hands of the country's authorities for personal gain. The religious leaders condemned Jesus for eating with tax collectors. After Matthew became a disciple, Jesus was with him often, and there is no indication that Matthew gave up his tax collecting. Maybe Jesus' nearly daily contact with Matthew caused the religious leaders to condemn him.

Simon was a Zealot. The Zealots were a fourth party in Judaism. (The other parties were the Pharisees, the Sadducees, and the Essenes.) The Zealots stood firmly for liberty and were prepared to face any kind of death for their country. They would undergo pain and were prepared to go to the length of secret murder and assassination in order to rid their country of foreign rule. Had Simon met Matthew anywhere other than in the company of Jesus, he would have considered him a traitor and killed him.[5]

Peter, Andrew, James, and John were two sets of fishermen brothers. Fishing was hard, strenuous work done by common laborers. Peter was eager to please and more than once promised more than he was willing to deliver. Andrew seemed to be willing to take second place and remained in the background. James and John had short fuses and were nicknamed "Sons of Thunder" (Mark 3:17).

Thomas was at the table. He consistently had questions about what was happening and why. He later refused to believe anything about the resurrection that was based on secondhand information.

As John related the events, Philip was one of the first disciples called. He introduced Nathanael to Jesus and assisted in feeding the five thousand. He had five daughters and later became an evangelist, according to tradition.

Bartholomew (or Nathanael), James the son of Alphaeus, and Thaddaeus also were at the table, but we know almost nothing about these three. Then there was Judas, who became identified as the betrayer. He was treasurer of the group, called by Jesus to be a disciple. He had potential, and there is no clear, ascertainable reason why he betrayed Jesus. Up to the very end Jesus reached out to Judas and kept the door open for change.

Do you recognize yourself in any of these disciples who were at the table? When we consider who was at the table the first time and who is at the table today, is the list really that different? Oh, the names have changed, but are not many of us unknowns, people in the background, ones who have jumped at the chance to call ourselves disciples of Christ and just as quickly jumped at opportunities to deny and betray the very One we claim to follow and emulate in our lives?

Through his attitude and action at the table during the last meal with his disciples, Jesus demonstrated that at this table everybody is welcome. That sounds nice to most of us, but we really don't come to the table with that attitude. Our private attitudes may be, "What is he doing here?" Or, "The nerve of some people to show up here and now." Or, "After the way she acted, I can't believe she would take communion."

There are tables where everybody isn't welcome. In the 1960s there were lunch counters where African Americans were prohibited to eat. There are still tables where African Americans, Hispanics, Arabs, Iranians, Jews, Germans, Japanese, or Russians are not welcome. But at God's table all are welcome.

You may choose to have a dinner party in your home. As the host or hostess you are free to invite whomever you wish. You may choose to exclude whomever you desire. It is your home, your table, and you are free to include or exclude anybody. But that is not permissible at God's table because it is not your table or my table or our table. Not one of us is the host or hostess at this table. This is God's table with God as the host. All are invited here. What a meal! What a prayer! What a life!

What happened at Jesus' last Passover meal has the potential of happening every time we place ourselves around any table. The highest cannot be spoken; it can only be acted. The grace of God may be acted at any meal and especially around the communion meal with its roots and framework deeply set in the Passover meal.

Jesus was forever extending God's love to people, letting them know it was never too late to make U-turns in life. There is a sense in which Jesus was saying to Judas, "You don't have to go through with this. It is not too late to change your mind." And Jesus says that to us every time we come to the table. Because every time we gather around the table, we are a motley group of followers, and every one of us has betrayed Christ who knows how many times since the last time we gathered around the table. But the invitation is still open. The offer is still made. As often as we come to the table, Jesus says, "Drink this cup. Eat this bread."

Jesus keeps praying the same prayer. He prayed his life, and nothing depicts it more clearly than this meal he shared with his disciples. He invites us to pray our lives in a similar way. He invites us to join him in his ministry of reconciliation. He invites us to make a New Covenant with him, to be his friends, to enflesh God's love in our lives. As we do we are engaged in praying our lives. We become the only Christs some people ever know. We become the enfleshment of God in the corner of the world where we live and work and play. We begin to pray our lives, and we learn how from Jesus who prayed his life. And all of it takes shape around a meal. What a meal! What a prayer! What living!

QUESTIONS TO PONDER

1. How can sharing a meal be a way of praying?
2. What distinctions would you make between offering a prayer and praying a life?
3. Is it too much of a stretch to suggest that the Passover meal symbolized Jesus praying his life? Why or why not?
4. What does it mean to you to think about praying your life?
5. How would you go about praying your life?
6. What would serve as the metaphor for praying your life as I have used the Passover meal as a metaphor for Jesus praying his life?

CHAPTER THREE

Who Am I?

LUKE 3:21–22

If we understand prayer only as words spoken directly to God, then we have very little information about prayer related to Jesus. We have the content of only twelve prayers of Jesus, and they are very brief except for one in John 17:1–26. Seven of them are one-liners spoken from the cross. However, if we understand prayer to be something of what the hymn writer said, "Prayer is the soul's sincere desire unuttered or expressed," then we have a great deal more about what prayer was like for Jesus and how he prayed.

Surely, Jesus prayed in the Temple on his first trip there. No doubt Jesus and his parents had prayed for a safe journey before they left Nazareth. Do you recall that Joseph and Mary left for their return to Nazareth without Jesus, apparently thinking he was in the caravan of travelers only to discover at dusk he wasn't there? Wonder what Jesus thought about God and prayer when night and day and night passed and he didn't know where Joseph and Mary were. Wonder if he thought God had not heard his prayer for a safe journey home. How safe could the journey be if he didn't even know where his parents were?

During the years between his twelfth and thirtieth birthdays, Jesus went to the Temple. Prayer was part of the worship of God in the Temple. Jesus must have prayed during those times. Between trips to the Temple he frequented the synagogue. He must have prayed there too. Surely, he prayed for his family, especially during and after the death of Joseph.

I say all of this because the first time the Gospels mention Jesus praying is in Luke's account of his baptism. Surely, that wasn't the first time Jesus ever prayed. Perhaps the writers assumed Jesus prayed at times like those I mentioned in the preceding paragraphs.

Luke wrote, "Now when all the people were baptized, and when Jesus also had been baptized and was praying, the heaven was opened" (3:21). Was Jesus praying before he was baptized, as he was being baptized, or after he was baptized, or was his baptism itself a prayer?

The early church spent bountiful energy backtracking the life of Jesus. The events in Jesus' life that the early church highlighted were not nearly as important as the interpretations given to the events. Thirty years after the resurrection of Christ, several people considered it worthwhile to write about some of the events that occurred in Jesus' life. His baptism is one of those events. Reporting the baptism of Jesus indicates its importance. Obviously, the event was important to Jesus, and he probably described the event to his disciples. No doubt that underscored the value of the event for the people who decided to compile written records of Jesus' life. It is reasonable to conclude that some of Jesus' family and friends witnessed his baptism and gave early followers their impressions and interpretations. In whatever manner the descriptions of this event were first formulated, the church has interpreted and reinterpreted the meaning of Jesus' baptism for twenty centuries.

To understand Jesus' baptism, how it was a prayer for him, and what the intent of this prayer was, we must examine the significance of the baptism of John the Baptist. All four Gospel writers recorded baptism being practiced by John, but only Matthew, Mark, and Luke recorded that John baptized Jesus. None of the Gospel writers gave us any information about the preparation of John the Baptist for his prophetic ministry. They told us nothing about his education, experience, or decision to preach and baptize. About all the facts we have are that his parents, Zechariah and Elizabeth, were old when he was born, his mother and Jesus' mother were cousins, and John was six months older than Jesus. Other information about John can be pieced together from knowledge and material unearthed in archaeological digs and discovered from sources describing events in Palestine during the first half of the first century C.E.

Each of the Gospel writers portrayed John as thundering out of the wilderness, stopping at the stony banks of the Jordan River to baptize those who would repent. You may have met some straitlaced people in your life, but I doubt if any were as straight and narrow as John the Baptist. John wore a camel's hair jacket with a leather belt, drank no wine, ate bugs and wild honey, and stayed in the desert as a recluse. Maybe the desert diet and heat caused him to come roaring into town breathing fire and brimstone. John must have been a sight to see, to smell, and to hear! Often he has been portrayed as an anger-filled man bellowing his message in a fashion that both intrigued and frightened his audience. When his listeners overheated from the guilt stirred by his message, John cooled them off by baptizing them in the Jordan River. His contemporary religious leaders said John was demon possessed.

I suspect that we have read John's life and his preaching with too much venom. From too many pulpits the only tone for the call to repentance, the only tone for change of direction in life, is anger. The tone of John's message was one of urgency but not necessarily one of anger or hatred. His voice was like that of Isaiah, a lonely one because it was the only one at the time calling for radical change. Does not the Word of God strike the ears of people with the force of a hint? The roar of John's message was not so much in its volume and tone as it was in its urgency.

I suspect that regardless of the content of his sermons, John delivered them with a tone of hope that listeners could and would change for the better. John's lifestyle, including his attire, his diet, and his spoken word, was part of his message. In Hebrew thought, word and deed were inseparable. To speak was to act and to act was to speak. Thus, Luke wrote that John preached a baptism of repentance.

Where did John get this idea of baptism? Had he been in the desert so long that his own body odor called for a bath? Did he conclude that the external cleansing he needed was symbolic of what everybody needed internally? Maybe that was part of John's thinking.

The Greek word *baptizo* means "to immerse." Josephus used the word to mean "to dye." The Christian Scriptures use *baptizo* only in the literal sense of "to dip in" (Luke 16:24; John 13:26). "Baptize" is used only in the cultic sense, infrequently of Jewish washings, and otherwise in the technical sense "to baptize." This usage suggests that baptism was considered something new and strange.[1]

Baptism was well known in the pagan world as the door through which people entered many of the mystery religions. There are early examples of sacral water ceremonies in Babylon, Persia, and India. The Ganges and Euphrates Rivers came to have a significance to Eastern religions comparable with that of the Jordan to Judaism and Christianity. The common root for these customs is impossible to unearth. Whether or not John knew about sacral water ceremonies and baptisms in other religions is unknown. It is probable that some who heard him preach were familiar with these practices.

The process for a proselyte, one not born a Jew, to enter Judaism included baptism. Three necessary elements were involved for non-Jews to enter Judaism: circumcision, baptism, and a sacrifice. The baptism was to be conducted in the presence of three witnesses. The candidates' nails and hair were cut and all of their clothing removed. They were immersed in water so that their bodies were totally covered. When they were raised out of the water, the essence of the law was read to them, they were warned of dangers and persecutions, and they confessed their sins to the fathers of their baptism. All of that was a means of acting out a total break with the past and was based on the many washings of the Jewish law for purification.[2]

By the first century C.E. Judaism was made up of four factions: Pharisees, Sadducees, Essenes, and Zealots. The Essenes are not mentioned by name in the biblical material. The Essenes' theological position was that they should withdraw from the world. They had a passion for cleanliness and were convinced that the only way to live and achieve cleanliness was to withdraw totally from the world and the influences of anyone other than their own Essenes. Further documentation of this group's existence and lifestyle has been substantiated in accounts of the Qumran community recorded in the Dead Sea Scrolls. It has been suggested that the Essenes might have taken in John the Baptist when his parents died or that John became influenced by them fairly early in his life. It is possible that he associated with and was influenced by the Essenes. Evidence is clear that if John associated with the Essenes, he also broke from them because it was only for themselves that they were preparing the way of God in the wilderness. John came out of the wilderness preaching a baptism of repentance. John might have been a straight-and-narrow man, but he was neither as rigid nor as isolationistic as the Essenes were.

There seems to be more than a coincidental connection between the demand of the Qumran community for holiness and the ethical demand of John. Both understood their demands to be internal ones, and the close connection of the two demands is expressed in the Manual of Discipline of the Qumran community: "No one is to go into the water in order to attain the purity of holy men. For men cannot be purified except they repent their evil."[3]

Although baptism was new neither to the Jews nor to many Gentiles, some characteristics about John's message made his message and his baptism distinctive. The prophetic voice had been silent in Judaism for nearly three hundred years. John's manner and style, dress and tone, were akin to those of the Hebrew prophets, especially Elijah. Thus, John's approach attracted attention. Elijah's loyalty to God resulted in his opposing the worship of Baal fostered by Jezebel. Elijah's memory had been preserved through Elisha and a guild of prophets. Later generations remembered the mystery of Elijah's translation through a whirlwind (2 Kings 2:11) and anticipated his return as the forerunner of the Day of God (Mal. 4:5). John's similarity to Elijah caused many to think he was Elijah. John denied that identity (John 1:21). Another distinctive aspect of John's preaching was his call to repentance. Periodically, a voice summoned Israel to repentance, and many people believed that if the nation would repent for one day, the Redeemer would arrive.

To that point, John had been preaching what had been preached before but with the renewed zeal, tone, and drama of a prophet.

However, when John tied baptism to repentance and called for Jews to be baptized to show that they had repented (Matt. 3:11), he interjected a completely new and disturbing concept into the religious climate. From John's perspective, everybody, Jews included, desperately needed the cleansing that God alone could give. John confronted the Pharisees and Sadducees, warning them that family names and pedigree exempted no one from accountability to God.

John's manner and message struck a responsive chord in the lives of people, and they flocked to the Jordan River to be baptized by him. One day Jesus was a part of the crowd who heard John preach. He stepped forward asking John to baptize him. John refused. Why? Had he and Jesus met previously? That is probable, but it is doubtful that they knew each other intimately. Jesus had been in Nazareth, apparently learning a carpenter's trade, and John had been in the desert robbing bees and eating bugs. Did John sense in Jesus a greatness that Jesus did not yet sense? Was John aware of some of Jesus' insights and inquisitiveness that began in the Temple but had been nurtured and cultivated throughout the intervening eighteen years? Was John so in awe of Jesus that he could not bring himself to baptize him?

Many would argue that John recognized Jesus as the Messiah or that he already knew Jesus was the Messiah before Jesus requested baptism. A major problem with this foreknowledge position is that later Matthew recorded (11:2–6) that John the Baptist sent some of his disciples to Jesus to ask him if he were the Coming One about whom John had preached or if they should look for another. If John were certain at baptism who Jesus was, why was he uncertain after being imprisoned? There is ample evidence that Jesus did not fit the messianic mold that people, including John the Baptist, cast for him. Apparently, John and his disciples had some doubts about Jesus.

It is evident that in his preaching John sounded a clear call for people to repent, for them to autograph their repentance by baptism, and John gladly baptized them. Exactly why John was stunned by Jesus' request for baptism is speculation because the Synoptic writers recorded only John's resistance. They did not interpret his resistance other than to identify John's feelings that Jesus should baptize him.

Jesus spoke a lasting word to John when he resisted baptizing Jesus. What Jesus said sliced through John's resistance. Jesus' encouragement to John to baptize him pointed toward cross bearing and cross living when he suggested that his baptism was "proper for us in this way to fulfill all righteousness" (Matt. 3:15).

Righteousness as a Hebraic concept is foreign to Western minds. The term is used in the context of relationships and refers to the demands made by relationships. The covenant relationship of people to God is primary in the Hebrew Scriptures. God would be their God if the Israelites would be God's people. Faith is the fulfillment of the relationship with God because faith is putting one's trust and confidence in God, the bedrock on which the covenant is built. God initiates relationship with people, and the relationship is consummated when people in faith promise themselves to God. The one who upholds the covenant relationship is identified as righteous. In this context God always is righteous because God consistently is faithful in keeping the promise to be our God, and we fulfill righteousness or complete the relationship when we are faithful to God.

Apparently, Jesus heard in John's message a clear and certain call for people to establish their relationship as the people of God. He acknowledged John's baptism as an appropriate sign of that covenant relationship. His statement that "it is proper for us in this way to fulfill all righteousness" might refer to himself and John or to himself and others who desired to be baptized by John.

Jesus' desire to fulfill righteousness was a prayer because he was expressing a faith commitment to God that by its very nature was a choice against ultimate loyalty to anything or anyone other than God. Later Jesus said it was impossible to serve two masters. To choose one was to choose against all others. To be faithful to God was to meet the demands of the relationship that fulfilled righteousness. John must have been convinced by Jesus' encouragement because he consented to baptize Jesus.

John's baptism of Jesus is beyond question, but it is not beyond problems. This event is a problem in the Gospels, and the authors made little or no effort to cover, excuse, or hide either the event or the problem that the event raises. Mark's might be the oldest Gospel, and in it he described John's baptism as one of repentance and he went on to say that Jesus was baptized by John. Mark had no record of John's resistance to Jesus' request to be baptized. The problem of Jesus' being baptized by John whose baptism signified repentance was not a problem for Mark. Perhaps his writing helped surface the issue. Luke briefly recorded that Jesus was baptized and was in prayer at the time. Matthew most acutely felt the problem of Jesus' being baptized by John. His record of John's refusal to baptize Jesus indicated Matthew's struggle. His struggle probably was indicative of the struggles that many of the followers of the Way were having with Jesus' baptism by 60 C.E.

The unanswered question is, Why was Jesus baptized by John? Since Jesus grew as a human being and faced life as a human being, it seems appropriate that his awareness of himself—who he was and who he hoped to be—was a gradual development that came through deepening awareness during his years in Nazareth. Is it possible that in hearing the preaching of John the Baptist, Jesus heard the word of God that struck a responsive chord in his life? Perhaps then he recognized that the opposite of repentance was to stay the course. He heard in John's word the clear call by which Israel could and must change the course. He sensed a new age was ushering in for his people and for the world, and John was sounding forth the call to people in a way that it had not been sounded for generations. Jesus saw this new age coming and sensed his desire and need to be part of it. Baptism was his prayer for the new age coming and for himself. He stepped forth to be baptized, signaling a beginning. He was praying for himself to be a partner with God in helping people experience new life, new direction, and new purpose. In that sense, Jesus redefined the form—baptism—as he later pointed out that when forms, old wineskins, had lost their usefulness and flexibility to carry the substance, new wine, the old wineskins should be thrown away and new wineskins should be used.

I wonder about the content of Jesus' prayer at his baptism. I would like to know, wouldn't you? The total event of Jesus' baptism was a prayer. It was a prayer addressing God, both questioning, "Who am I?" and stating, "Who I am." His baptism was the climax of a long period of reflection, inner struggle, and deepening insight. Jesus' baptism was his public commitment to God that he would strive to love the world for God's sake. Just how Jesus arrived at that conviction and just when he decided to make that commitment through baptism remain a mystery. With such serious examination of his life, is it not appropriate that Jesus would approach his baptism in an attitude of prayer? Jesus was in communion with God about his life and how he was going to live his life. Only Luke suggests a connection between Jesus' baptism and his praying. Is it possible that Jesus' baptism was Jesus' prayer about the direction of his life?

An integral part of any concern about the direction of one's life is the essential question, "Who am I?" It is a question every human being asks in some form. In a sense an answer really cannot be given to this question. The best a person can do is to tell others the direction in which he or she is marching. "Who am I?" is an appropriate question and prayer to address to God. It is a way of seeking understanding about what it means to be created in the image of God.

Jesus had been addressing his question to God for some time as he searched and sought clarity about how he would live his life. Being baptized was a way for Jesus to act out his resolution and his answer to the question. His baptism signified the completion of his covenant with God, saying to God and to himself, "This is the direction I am going." At his baptism the anchor was lifted, the cables were cut, and Jesus' life set sail into the deep, charting a direct and difficult course. It was a course that he knew not every turn or every event, but it was a direction toward which he chose to move. Jesus might have been as surprised as anybody at what was happening to him. Jesus' baptism was a way for him to act out that he was praying his life. It was a way for him to open his life to God, commit his living in a direction, and trust God to be a constant guide, companion, and friend.

Jesus' baptism was an outward, visible sign of his commitment to ministry. The Synoptic Gospels have a similar sequence of events: the preaching of John the Baptist, the baptism of Jesus, Jesus' sojourn in the wilderness, the calling of disciples, and the expansion of ministry. The Synoptic writers intentionally portrayed the ministry of Jesus as beginning at his baptism.

Not only did Jesus' baptism inaugurate his ministry, but it also revealed its unexpected nature. Jesus interpreted his baptism as turning away from the status quo and turning toward self-denial that led all the way to Golgotha. Jesus called people to die. Jesus used the word "baptism" to refer to his own impending death (Mark 10:38). He redefined the form and suggested that baptism is not as much the water that washes as it is the flood that drowns.

In the biblical record of the early church, baptism was a prayer acting out before God and other believers that the one being baptized was dying to the old life in sin and rising to a new life in Christ. Baptism signals a reshaping and redirecting of one's thinking because of the impact that the awareness of God's presence has had on one's life. Baptism is an act of commitment and promise in which the old life is buried and the believer is raised to a new life—new in direction, purpose, and objective. Baptism is an outward, visible sign of the inward, invisible grace of God at work in a person's life. Baptism serves as a seal of the promise of God's love, care, and presence. There is no recorded instance in the Christian Scriptures of the baptism of any persons other than new converts. Baptism is a way of praying, "I am ready to grow. I willingly entrust myself to God's creative power to grow me beyond where I am." Baptism became a way of expressing the soul's sincere desire. Thus, baptism has become the signal of the dawning of a person's faith in God, which completes the covenant relationship.

Baptism marks the dividing line between the old and the new. It is a signal that a person is beginning a faith commitment to God just as Jesus' baptism signaled the beginning of his faith commitment to ministry. A person does not know at the beginning of a journey all that is in store on the way. Jesus did not know all that would unfold during his ministry. He had no idea that his disciples would have such a difficult time learning or that religious leaders would be so resistant to change. The difficulty and resistance continue with disciples today.

If you pray like Jesus, life will not be trouble free, I promise you. Actually, you may be surrounded by trouble much of the time. If you pray like Jesus, you may have some enemies, but I promise you, you won't be without a Friend. If you pray like Jesus, you may experience doubt, but I promise you, you won't be overtaken by despair. If you pray like Jesus, you may get badly hurt, but I promise you, you won't be destroyed. I hope you will spend some time reflecting on your baptism as praying like Jesus. You may be surprised at the peace and purpose you begin to experience.

QUESTIONS TO PONDER

1. If you have been baptized, how was your baptism a prayer?
2. How was your baptism "praying like Jesus"?
3. If you began today reflecting and reinterpreting your baptism as praying your life like Jesus prayed his, what changes in your life would be the result?
4. How does your baptism address the question "Who am I?"
5. Write a prayer that expresses the meaning of your baptism as praying to God.

CHAPTER FOUR

What Am I to Do?

LUKE 4:1–13

Prayer is the communication system between a person and God. More than words and activities, prayer is the center of one's being, seeking to be in touch with and in tune with God.

One of the most powerful prayers of Jesus is popularly known as his temptation experience in the wilderness. Matthew, Mark, and Luke each reported about the experience. Each writer noted that Jesus was alone in the wilderness for forty days.

If baptism was Jesus' prayer about being, then his wilderness temptation experience was his prayer about doing. Someone has said that prayer is a trialogue where "my best self and my worst self talk to each other and God is a listening participant." This is descriptive of Jesus' wilderness experience. He was wrestling with how he was going to live out who he had identified himself to be. Several options presented themselves to him, and his temptations were expressions of the praying he did about this issue in his life.

Jesus went into the wilderness to explore and formulate both how he would minister and what his methods of ministry would be. It is no accident in telling about the life of Jesus that the wilderness temptations are included. They illustrate his humanity. The issues of security, power, and popularity surface for Jesus in the wilderness. The way Jesus faced each of these issues instructs us about how we can negotiate the struggles raised for us by similar temptations.

If the only words we had about temptation were "Lead us not into temptation" (Matt. 6:13), then many would conclude that God does the tempting. Some hold this view and substantiate it with the event in Abraham's life when he prepared to sacrifice Isaac. That event has been interpreted as a time of temptation and testing by God.

The portion of Adam and Eve's story identified as the Fall, however, locates the source of temptation with the serpent. The serpent is distinctly different and separate from God. Jesus, in the account of his temptations and testing struggles in the wilderness, reported that the evil one sought to seduce him into taking shortcuts. The evil one is separate and apart from God.

Diabolos means "obstructor," "that which opposes." It is an opposing force that has power. *Diabolos* is translated "devil" and means "adversary" or "one who is the antithesis of God."[1] Many people support dualism, the forces of good and evil having equal strength, with the edge going to evil in this life and to good in the next life. Nowhere in the Hebrew Scriptures is this the concept of evil. In the book of Job, Satan acted more as an accuser or the prosecuting attorney. In First Chronicles, the common noun used for Satan denoted virtually a personification of human frailty. A person had a weakness that was personified and called Satan. That was what Jesus did later when he said to Peter, "Get behind me, Satan!" (Mark 8:33).

What obstructs a person from serving God and communicating the love of God may be identified as evil, the devil, or Satan. Satan is a name given to a spirit that is nameless with which a person may collaborate. The principal weapon of Satan is fear, and the primary methodology is the use of half-truths. Collaboration with Satan results in misused or abused freedom that obstructs life and therefore obstructs the presence of God. Scott Peck draws two conclusions about Satan that are helpful at this point: (1) Satan has no power except in a human body; and (2) the only power that Satan has is through human belief in its lies.[2] These two conclusions highlight the difficulty in knowing where the person, especially the subconscious, leaves off and Satan begins. Thus, obstructor is descriptive of Satan.

The Greek verb *peirazein,* translated "to tempt," has a different connotation. The basic force of this verb connotes testing with the intent to build up and make stronger. In this sense, temptation is an invitation and opportunity for growth. Olympic athletes illustrate this. Their training is much more demanding than any competitive event can ever be. Strength and stamina have to be developed, and this can be done only by putting themselves "to the test" with a workout that is more strenuous than they will face in competition.

It is correct that testing is a part of life. It is incorrect that testing is what God does to find out how strong or how weak we are. To hold that testing occurs to educate God flies in the face of the assertion that God already knows about us. Surely, the One who knows the number of hairs on our heads also knows the pressure points of our emotional stability.

As Jesus told his disciples about his wilderness temptation experience, he said that being human involved searching out one's limitations. In this search a person may try to be more or less than she was created to be. To go either direction is to sin. Perhaps Jesus had this view in mind when he said that straight is the way and narrow is the gate that leads into the realm of God.

We routinely fail to do the best of which we are capable. With each failure we wrong God, our neighbors, and ourselves. Constantly before us are invitations to yield to our desires, but these invitations are not extended by God. Evidently, Paul understood this to be true of life. He wrote to the Corinthian Christians that the difficulties they were experiencing were common (1 Cor. 10:13). He added that God was the resource who enabled people to deal with hardship and who gave them strength not to sin.

Life is filled with temptations, and we cannot avoid them. To live life is to be confronted with choices. Temptations do not come from God so that God may know the stuff of which we are made. God already knows. Temptations afford us opportunities to grow or chances to regress, depending upon our decisions. A temptation is a crisis. In the Chinese language two characters meaning danger and opportunity are united to form the word "crisis." A temptation is a dangerous opportunity. Whether it is a danger or an opportunity depends upon how we respond to the temptation. We must evaluate where the path of each temptation seems to lead and determine the direction we need to move in order to be faithful and consistent in our commitment to God.

Tradition has implied that Jesus experienced only three temptations, although Luke wrote that the evil one left Jesus for a season. Jesus was confronted with numerous temptations throughout his life, but maybe all of them were variations on the three Jesus wrestled with and prayed his way through in the wilderness. Serious consideration of Jesus' wilderness temptations reveals that they were growth opportunities for him. Jesus' wilderness endeavor was one of personal struggle. Insight into how Jesus dealt with temptations may best be examined by studying the Gospel accounts of his wilderness temptations. Since Jesus was in the wilderness alone, he must have been the source for the information about the experience.

Because Jesus clearly committed himself to be a servant who would love the world for God's sake, his experience in the wilderness was a time of prayer and soul-searching as he raised the question with God, "What am I to do?" How was Jesus to live out his commitment of love for God and human beings? It was a lonely struggle. Lonely struggles often have the feeling of being deserted. No doubt while Jesus wrestled with what he was going to do, being in a deserted place was symbolic of his deserted emotional feeling. During his struggles, Jesus became increasingly aware that he was alone with the Alone. He discovered that he was not all by himself in the journey. At the deepest, most intense level of struggle and search, Jesus experienced God caring for him and giving him guidance, instruction, and support. What a powerful prayer experience!

As Jesus asked God, "What am I to do?" several options presented themselves to him. The options came in the forms of the issues of security, power, and popularity. The way Jesus faced each issue instructs us in what praying like Jesus is like and how praying like Jesus can help us deal with the same issues.

To live life is to be confronted with choices. So it was for Jesus. He was seeking direction to the question, "How do I bring people to God and God to people?" That was the mission to which he committed himself at his baptism. After making his commitment, he then sought routes to take in accomplishing the mission. Thus, Jesus spent time in the wilderness.

As Jesus wandered in the wilderness, he wondered how he could persuade people to turn their lives toward God. He was communing with God about how to get people to follow God. A natural method came to mind—food. Why wouldn't he think of food? He had been fasting for a long period of time. His fasting stirred his hunger, and the stones around him reminded him of bread. Jesus breathed a prayer: "Aha! That is the way to bring people to God: give them bread."

An aspect of arrogance is evident in Jesus' thoughts of food as the means to get people to come to God. This can be a way to help us discern between God's guidance and our own impulses. Jesus' initial reaction was to give no thought to limits at all, to exercise his strength and use his power with no regard for any concern except himself. Jesus thought that if he were doing what God wanted him to do, perhaps he could bypass the laws of reality that included planting, cultivating, reaping, grinding, and cooking. Right in the middle of Jesus' effort to communicate with God was the temptation to disregard the limitations of being human.

The first temptation contained double trouble offering a shortcut to security in bringing people to God. First, it was bribery. To offer bread to people in exchange for their willingness to come to God was to obtain followers for the sake of what they would get out of it. God calls people to a life of giving rather than getting. Too many modern testimonies are filled with descriptions of material possessions, accomplishments, and successes. The implication is direct and clear that the testifiers are propagating their payoff for following God. People are saying, "See what we got for following God." Authentic disciples may receive crucifixion from discipleship.

The second mistake in the shortcut of security is that it deals with symptoms rather than the cause itself. Providing bread for hungry people is an emergency measure to keep them from starving; however, it is only a first step. To do nothing more is to make people who are hungry more dependent and indebted while the causes of hunger and other insecurities run rampant, ravaging the lives of millions across the globe.

As Jesus prayed for God's help, his first thoughts were to be a cheap leader, to begin with security rather than to end with it; to bring outer abundance rather than inner holiness and wholeness. In telling the story of temptation, Jesus laid himself bare, letting people see and feel his struggles and agony and, in essence, hear his prayers. Jesus concluded that the shortcut of security was destructive to his objective of bringing God to people and people to God. Jesus came to that conclusion because he stayed with his conversation with God long enough to realize that his initial reaction was incongruent with who God was and how God cares for people.

On other occasions when Jesus prayed and sought God's guidance, the shortcut of security reared its head to offer itself: when the Pharisees asked for a sign of his being the Child of God; when the high priest chided him to save himself; when the thief said, "Save yourself and us." Apparently, through his communion with God in the wilderness, Jesus gained strength and insight for dealing with the shortcut of security. When we pray about the direction of our lives and what we are to do in loving the world for God's sake, we can be assured that our security rests in relationship with God rather than in immediate gratification.

When he communed with God about what he was to do, Jesus wrestled with the issue of power. He knew he had power. All people do. The struggle for Jesus was how to use power to achieve his calling and objective in life. One temptation was to become the type of Messiah the world expected.

The word "power" is of Latin derivation, from a word meaning "to be able." Power is the ability to effect change, and it is not of itself good or evil. The use one makes of power determines its moral quality. The Hebrew Scriptures have a consistent image of power that portrays God's creative and fulfilling energy. This energy is activated in the worshiper of God and through the worshiper to his or her societal situation.

Danger was appealing to Jesus. There was something adventuresome about the possibility of drawing many people together. In addition to that appeal, Jesus had been commissioned as the right leader at his baptism. Envisioning the kingdoms of the world, Jesus hungered for them. How he wished he might draw all of them together as servants of God. There was plausibility in Jesus' feeling that he could accomplish almost anything and that he had the power to do whatever he chose. This is the struggle every child of God faces: to overreach our limits and be less than God created us to be.

On the threshold of his ministry, Jesus was confronted with the end of his ministry and what means he would use to achieve the end. Many people have concluded that as long as the end toward which they are moving is basically good, they ought not concern themselves with how they get there. Invariably, this attitude deadens people's sensitivity to their ethical responsibility, and they conclude that the best way to get along is to go along.

This second temptation in Luke's account is a description of the power struggle that was alive in Jesus as he prayed to God, seeking to know what he was to do. It is the same type of power struggle that confronts us as we pray. It is illustrated in the actions of the two Adolfs of the Nazi Party in Germany in World War II.[3] Apparently, Adolf Hitler had incredible arrogance. He saw himself as a superhuman destined to rule the world like a god. He believed himself to be above all rules that applied to other people. He could break treaties, annihilate a whole race of people, and attempt by sheer power to impose his ruling hand over others. Adolf Hitler epitomized the arrogant side of the power struggle.

Adolf Eichmann was on the apathetic side. He was the official in charge of the final solution of the Jewish problem. Years later, when he was tracked down and put on trial for crimes against humanity, his only defense for his part in the atrocity was that he was doing what he was told to do! He defined himself as a cog in the machine—just one more bureaucrat who received from above and passed on below. He accepted no responsibility whatsoever for his part in the process. In these two Adolfs is a modern embodiment of the alternatives that Jesus faced in the loneliness of the desert.

Too often when people are in the midst of a crisis, they are confronted with the necessity of a decision and feel bound by either/or alternatives. On many occasions people, especially religious leaders, cornered Jesus with either/or alternatives. Invariably, Jesus chose a third option as his solution to the issue. That was what he did with the question of how to use his power. He was tempted to choose either arrogance or apathy. As he communed with God, Jesus chose to walk the corridor between arrogance and apathy by joining his power with the power of God and the power of others for their benefit, not counting the cost to himself. Not only in the wilderness, but also on other occasions, Jesus evaded the shortcut of misused or abusive power by walking the straight, narrow path between arrogance and apathy.

Jesus strolled through the wilderness feeling the sand under his feet and the sun burning on his brow. He reflected upon his baptism and gave serious consideration to who he was and what he was going to do. Jesus began to think through some possible approaches to communicate that he was the Child of God and to consider the message he would bring to people. Jesus used his imagination. Isn't this one of the ways we work on a solution to an issue? Isn't imagination an excellent method of praying? We are confronted by an issue, and part of our communion with God is to play out in our minds various alternatives to assist us in deciding on direction. So was the approach for Jesus. He imagined himself on the porch of the Temple looking down into the Kidron Valley, 450 feet below. He envisioned many people gathered on the Temple grounds, as occurred during holy days. Jesus thought to himself, *The people need to know who I am. Perhaps if I jump from this porch, attention will be drawn to me. I need to get people's attention in order for them to listen to me.* Jesus understood that the Messiah was to come through the Temple, and that seemed an opportune way of coming through the Temple to the people.

In thinking of his leap for attention, Jesus recalled part of Psalm 91: "'God will command the angels concerning you, to protect you,' and 'On their hands they will bear you up, so that you will not dash your foot against a stone'" (Luke 4:10–11). Note the half-truth that is expressed by extracting a verse out of context. How often we take this approach! The context in which this part of the psalm is set is the promise of God to be with people and protect them as events and circumstances happen over which they have no control. The context is not that of deliberately jeopardizing their lives so that God can rescue them.

When we want to travel in a specific direction in life but are struggling with the decision, we may find a passage of Scripture to support our desire. At this juncture in Jesus' life he was tempted to twist the Word of God to fit his desire. Maybe if he did leap from the porch, God would take hold of him and place him safely in the valley below. People would see the sensational feat and be drawn to him, he imagined. But Jesus prayed and thought further before he jumped. He concluded, "The sensational of today becomes the commonplace of tomorrow, and I would have to do ever more sensational feats to keep people with me." Jesus resisted the sensational approach of playing to the gallery.

There was another reason why Jesus refused to play to the gallery. His faith and commitment to God called for him to take risks and assured him that God would journey with him. Nevertheless, Jesus saw the foolishness of putting himself in a destructive situation just to see if God would protect him from his own foolishness. Risk taking is to be done on the basis of confirmed faith, not as an intention to remove doubt so that faith can be confirmed.

Jesus was tempted toward the sensational as a means to draw instant followers. Rather than rushing toward that temptation, Jesus stepped back from it, looked at it carefully, and saw an opportunity for growth for himself and those who would come after him. In his communion with God, Jesus concluded that he should not tempt the Sovereign God. That awareness negated the understanding that God was at anyone's beck and call.

Jesus considered the shortcut of popularity. He thought of at least one way to receive instant, positive response, but he also saw the shallowness of the approach and the temporariness of such a response. He realized that such a leap could be a leap to his death. He rejected the shortcut of popularity and chose instead the long route of service.

Jesus was eager to minister to people and to draw them to God, but he resisted quick fixes and superficial methods to accomplish his task.

An early event in my life was instructive to me later in understanding Jesus' resistance to shortcuts. Robert Percy was my fifth grade Sunday school teacher, a fine man, the father of four beautiful daughters (I noticed later), but he was a lifeless teacher. I remember only one statement he made, "The longest way around is the shortest way home." The statement raised more questions than it provided answers, and so I filed it away under "Confusing Statements That Don't Make Sense." It was a year later that the confusion was cleared from the statement. I was invited to Ronnie Shearer's birthday party. Ronnie's parents took us to the picture show. After the movie, we began our walk to Ronnie's house for cake and ice cream. We were in view of his house when we came to a fork in the road. The long way was to the left, but the short route was to the right and went down by the creek. Being intelligent boys, knowing that three heads were better than one, we chose the shortcut by way of the creek. When we arrived at the creek, numerous things beckoned—rocks to be skipped across the water, puddles to wade, frogs to catch. Who knows how long it took us to get across the creek. We lost track of time. Eventually, we crossed the creek and headed up to Ronnie's house. As we approached the house, I saw my parents in the front yard. First, I wondered what they were doing there. In amazement I thought, *Surely, it isn't time for the party to be over.* Then, I realized, *Howard, the party is over for you!* Was it ever! That day, the longest way around would have been the shortest way home for me.

Jesus took the long way around, and what he got out of it was a cross. We need to be aware of that when we talk about praying like Jesus. Praying like Jesus can help us to realize that Jesus did not conclude that whatever came to mind as he sought God's guidance was necessarily from God or was God's instruction. The shortcuts that Jesus resisted are excellent examples.

In the best sense of the statement "The way of the cross leads home," the way of the cross is that of service, giving oneself, spending one's life for the express purpose of demonstrating and manifesting the love of God. When this is done, the shortcuts of security, power, and popularity are resisted. Jesus' forty-day wilderness journey was an extended time of communing with God. It was a time when he offered to God the various options that came to his mind of how he could go about his ministry. Through his dialogue with God, Jesus discovered that the first options that came to him were shortcuts that would short-circuit the meaning and message of God's love. Through his prayers in the wilderness, Jesus gained insight, wisdom, and strength to resist the shortcuts. Then he had a clear focus of the shape and direction his ministry would take.

The decisions Jesus made were not once-and-for-all decisions. There were various times during his ministry when Jesus revisited the options of shortcuts. By keeping the lines of communication constantly open with God, Jesus explored the options with God and resisted the shortcut options throughout his ministry. No doubt Jesus' communion with God in the wilderness set the tone for his constant relationship with God. His constant prayer seemed to be this: "How can I bring God to the people and the people to God? How can I love the world for God's sake?" The result of his communion with God was that he continually demonstrated the longest way around was the shortest way home. If we pray like Jesus, we, too, will discover the longest way around is the shortest way home.

Perhaps every temptation that Jesus faced and that we encounter is a variation of the temptation of security, power, or popularity. A closer, more serious examination of the Gospel accounts of Jesus' life reveals many opportune times arose when the obstructor offered Jesus a shortcut. Each time Jesus responded by taking the long view and traveling the long way because he was committed to loving the world for God's sake. In every situation in which a shortcut was an option, Jesus chose the long way, because when love for God is the bottom line, the longest way around is the shortest way home. Jesus' temptation experiences in the wilderness were powerful opportunities for him to commune with God about how he was going to live his life.

QUESTIONS TO PONDER

1. How does thinking about Jesus' wilderness temptations as prayer affect you?
2. How does such an approach alter the way you have thought about these events in Jesus' life?
3. Do you agree that all temptations are variations on security, power, and popularity?
4. What are some examples when you have been tempted to take the shortcuts of security, power, and popularity in being who you understand God wants you to be?
5. How are temptations you experience occasions for you to commune with God?
6. What is most comforting about considering Jesus' temptation experiences as prayers?
7. What is most disturbing about considering Jesus' temptation experiences as prayers?

CHAPTER FIVE

The Learner's Prayer

MATTHEW 6:5–15

I'm confident Jesus prayed before he read the scripture and spoke in the synagogue in Nazareth as he began his ministry. Remember how he was treated there? He was rejected, and some people even wanted to kill him. Surely, he prayed about the choices for his apostles. The ones he chose didn't turn out to have outstanding attributes or wonderful attitudes. All of them seemed a bit rough around the edges and unpolished in the center. James and John argued over who would be the greatest in the realm of God. Peter denied knowing Jesus, and Judas betrayed him. Results like that raise questions about Jesus' prayer life.

Therein is part of our difficulty. Our questions disclose our expectations and biases. Our evaluation of many situations is, What are the results? What is in it for me? What will I get out of this? So it is with prayer. We evaluate the value and worth of prayer based on results—do we get what we asked for? Many interpret answered prayer as having received what they prayed for, and if they did not receive what they wanted and prayed for, they conclude God did not answer their prayers. Garth Brooks puts a popular spin on this result with his recording "Thank God for Unanswered Prayer."

An amazing assertion is made in the Gospels. According to the Gospel writers, Jesus' disciples asked him to teach them only one thing. Does that surprise you? I would have expected them to ask him to teach them all kinds of things. I would have expected them to ask Jesus to teach them to cast out demons or to be able to make blind persons to see or deaf people to hear. My supposition is that they would have asked Jesus to teach them how to change water into wine or how to walk on water. But they didn't ask him any of those things. The only thing they asked Jesus to teach them was to pray (Luke 11:1–4).

There must have been something in the way Jesus prayed, when he prayed, why he prayed, or what he prayed for that influenced his disciples. Otherwise, of the unlimited number of things the disciples could have asked Jesus to teach them, why is the only request they made of which we have written record, "Teach us to pray"?

And do you know how Jesus taught them to pray? He gave them an example of a prayer. Although it is popularly known as the Lord's Prayer, it is better to identify it as the Model Prayer, the Disciple's Prayer, or better yet, the Learner's Prayer. The prayer we repeat as the Lord's Prayer, the only prayer of Jesus known by some people, serves as an illustration and a model for the learner, one seeking to learn to pray.

The Learner's Prayer suggests that we are to communicate three things to God when we pray like Jesus: respect for God, desire for the will and reign of God to take place, and daily needs. Elton Trueblood has suggested that we soak ourselves in this prayer and then pray freely.[1]

The Learner's Prayer has two sections: the "you" section and the "us" section. The "you" section addresses God and the disciple's respect for God. The "us" section deals with the disciple's daily needs and is identified by some as the petition section.[2]

The first thing Jesus suggests in the Learner's Prayer is that we address God as someone who knows us, loves us, and cares about us. Jesus addressed God as a loving parent and friend. The fact he said, "Abba," encourages us to use an intimate term when we address God. Jesus teaches the freedom and marvelous possibility of addressing the God of the universe as a loving, caring, protecting, providing, disciplining parent, as a father or mother.[3]

I wonder if Jesus gave the disciples this entire example of prayer in one sitting or if he gave it to them a phrase at a time? There is no way to know. Maybe when they asked him to teach them to pray, he said,

"Well, start with 'our Abba.'" Perhaps that was all he suggested for several days or weeks. Jesus' use of a personal, intimate word for God is quite a contrast to his ancestors who did not, would not, have a word for God. Our language development has resulted in words that serve as vocal pictures for us. In the ancient Hebrews' way of thinking, God was so vast, so much other than human beings, that they would speak no word to represent God. The closest they got was the combination of four consonants, YHWH. Later, vowels were added, and the Hebrew name for God eventually came to be Yahweh, a strange-sounding name to our ears.

Note that in Jesus' instruction on praying, it is "our Abba," not "my Abba" or "your Abba." Jesus was being clear that no one person or group had a corner on addressing God, getting God's attention, or gaining God's favor. However, God was to be understood as close, personal, intimate, loving, caring Parent/Friend. Jesus said to address God in terms that convey the closest intimacy you can imagine with one who loves you deeply, knows you better than you know yourself, and wants to be like a wise friend and guiding parent of grown, mature children.

How has your relationship with your parents changed as you have aged? Are there times when you collaborate with one or both of your parents about decisions? This is not a relationship in which you are being told what to do. For that matter, through the years we have learned that approach has never been the best parenting. The healthiest parenting happens when parents work with their children from the first days of life to guide and help them make decisions on their own. That is the meaning of this proverb: "Train children in the right way, and when old, they will not stray" (Prov. 22:6). Help children find the direction of their lives, help them identify and know their gifts and innate abilities, and continually guide them in developing in the direction these lead. When they are older, they will be clear about who they are and how they want to live their lives. Their contributions as partners with God will be numerous, vast, and generous, as God's contributions have been to them.

Maybe Jesus was bringing his disciples through stages of relationship with God so that they could come to have a proper understanding of God through a life of prayer. If that is true, then maybe the first stage is like talking with kinfolks and addressing God as Abba.[4]

Matthew set the Learner's Prayer in the context of the Sermon on the Mount. Surely, the Sermon on the Mount is a collection of Jesus' teachings that the early followers put together rather than one sermon given one time for his disciples' hearing and learning. Maybe the Learner's Prayer was given a phrase at a time for the disciples to live with for several days before they considered anything further. What would happen to you if you lived with each phrase in the Learner's Prayer for a few days before you considered, thought about, or prayed the next part of the prayer?

What does it mean to address God as "our Abba"? I would add that with the intimate term "Abba," we can address God as our Mother and Father, or Baba, as Jessie does in John Killinger's novels. The point is that we develop an intimate relationship with God and then use a name to address God that conveys the intimacy and the inclusiveness of being in relationship with God. "The intimacy between parent and child is not the intimacy of friends or lovers on equal terms. Parents routinely will know more, overlook more, care more, fret more, provide more, than anyone else of a person's acquaintance."[5] Thus, we address God as our Mother and Father. To say "our Abba" is to acknowledge that all of us are children of God, all of us are created by God. If that is our relationship with God, then our relationship with one another is as brothers and sisters. To start praying "our Abba" changes the images in our minds. The changed images reflect our connectedness and our interdependence.

How we address God says something about our respect for God. Respect for God has fallen on hard times, at least in part because of the idolatrous notion in our culture that we are self-made people. Nothing is farther from the truth.

Human beings can do amazing things, and the evidence is revealed in many areas—medicine, space travel, city skyscrapers. Our tendency is to marvel at the wonders of people and be oblivious of the greater wonders God has created. I have a fascination with the ocean. I am amazed how the mixture of sand, sky, salt water, and sea breeze can cleanse my being. Whenever I am at the beach, I position myself at least once so that nothing human-made is in sight. I become engulfed, awed, and as Sidney Lanier said, "I'll build me a nest on the greatness of God."[6]

Our respect for God leads us to desire and want what God wants. We then can pray that God's will and reign will come in the world through our lives. The will of God is for people to love God and human beings. Whenever we love God and love others as ourselves, we are doing the will of God.

After the disciples had chewed on and thought every thought they knew to think about "our Abba," Jesus suggested they say, "Our Abba in heaven." First, there is this intimate closeness, close as kinfolks, close as Mommy and Daddy, and then, there is this distance, farawayness, heaven. What does that mean, "in heaven"? We think of it as a place no one has ever come from to tell us what it's like. We often talk about people going there, but those who go there are never heard from again and eventually are forgotten about except now and then. When we are reminded of them, there is a drop or flood of sadness in our memory, depending on the day and what is remembered. And what have we heard from heaven? Absolutely nothing except silence—deep, dark, eerie silence. Does God care? Is God there?

Jesus told his disciples that if they wanted to learn to pray, they needed to be communing with a God who was as close as their moms and dads but could not be seen or touched or heard except in the eyes of the wise, in the hands of the compassionate, and in the voices of children. And Jesus just left it there. He and the disciples continued walking. The disciples were shaking their heads, trying to clear them so they could wrap their minds around this close-distant God who seemed to have made such a difference to Jesus. They wanted to know how to relate to this One, and the little bit Jesus had offered them had boggled their minds. Everything was a lot clearer before they had asked for prayer instructions and before Jesus took them seriously and started instructing.

Eventually, they got this out of their minds and were mentally moving on to other things when Jesus brought it up again. He said, "Remember the other day I urged you to pray, 'Our Abba in heaven'?

Well, there is more. Now pray, 'Our Abba in heaven, hallowed be your name.'" This God who is as close and personal as breathing and who is far beyond us—distant and silent—also is sacred. We are to hallow this One's name. God's name stretches to the other side of the street, the other side of the world, the other side of the universe. God's name is set aside as important, sacred, no other name like this one. This is separation but not estrangement. This God is beyond but not foreign. This God was so sacred that ancestors like Abraham never uttered a name for God. When Moses tried to figure out who this God was that was calling him to go to Pharaoh, all Moses could come up with was "I Am that I Am." God is. God is God. Period. Here you and I are thousands of years later. Who knows how many words have been used to talk about God, but the only thing that Moses said or Jesus said or we can say with any certainty is God is God.

Next, Jesus urged the disciples to ask for God's reign to come on earth. He instructed them to pray for the reign and will of God to be done in this world as they are done in heaven. To pray like Jesus is to want the reign of God to come on earth. I suspect our first impressions of God's reign on earth are much like a reign of wishes. We wish the world were better, safer, kinder, gentler, fairer. Our first thoughts of God's realm on earth are of a world with a little more fairness and justice around the edges. We probably see God's realm as the prototype of the nation in which we live. We in the United States project that the realm of God on earth would be something like the ultimate, perfect democracy.

What if God's reign did come on earth? What would that be like? Do we have any idea what we are praying will happen? Do we assume that God's realm would be without crime? If crime were abolished, could we survive? What about all of those police officers out of work? Lawyers would have no one to defend. Prison doors would swing open and cells would empty. We would not need any more laws written, so Congress could be abolished. We would not need the executive branch of the government, so the president could turn out the lights at the White House and go home. There would be no need to interpret laws, so all the judges could find other jobs. I don't know about God's reign coming on earth. Our whole economy would be shattered.

There would be no war and no rumors of war, so we could shut down the Pentagon and the CIA, the military academies and bases. We could close the munitions factories. Send all the military personnel home. Where would we put all the people, thousands of them returning from Europe, the Middle East, and the Pacific?

Surely, in God's realm everyone would be healthy. There go the hospitals, nursing homes, orderlies, nurses, doctors, physicians' assistants. There go health insurance and prescription drugs and pharmacists. I'm not sure we're ready for this or have really thought about what it means to pray, "Your realm come. Your will be done, on earth as it is in heaven."

Actually, the realm of God has already come. It came rushing in with Jesus. God's realm and the realm of this world are locked in battle. To pray for God's realm to come is to take sides. It is to say we want God's realm to win. It is to say we are placing our lives, our energy, and our abilities at God's disposal. To pray like this is to commit ourselves to be ministers of reconciliation. Maybe this why we mumble this prayer. We memorize it and say it quietly and quickly so no one will hear it, hoping God won't hear it. We don't hear it, because if we hear it, if we pay attention to what we are saying, we will be making some changes. Maybe that is why we want to call this the Prayer of Jesus—then it isn't ours—we don't have any ownership in it; it is someone else's prayer. Maybe the worst thing we could have done was to make this prayer so familiar and say it so often in unison in worship.

Jesus was urging his disciples to have the attitude and intention in their praying that are evident behind the content of this prayer. We are to pray in such a way that we are taking sides. We are praying that the realm of God will win. Actually, the realm of God has already won. The decision to be made is whether we are going to choose to be on the side of the realm of God or the realm of the world.

God's realm is not a political entity with a geographical location. When Jesus instructed his disciples to pray for the realm of God to come, he meant that we are to request and desire some changes in ourselves. That involves struggle, difficulty, and hard work. We would much prefer for God's realm to go rather than to come.

Once "Your realm come. Your will be done, on earth as it is in heaven" becomes our prayer, our sincere desire, then we move from the "you" part to the "us" part of praying. The "us" part of the Learner's Prayer is characterized by verbs in the imperative mood. The imperative mood is one of commanding another what to do. Three verbs dominate this section: "give," "forgive," and "rescue." These three verbs clearly indicate the awareness that God is the Creator and Sustainer of life. I wish we had a recording of Jesus saying this prayer. Somehow I don't think the routine, matter-of-fact way that we often repeat this prayer is the way Jesus suggested that his disciples pray.

Have you ever thought of praying like Jesus as telling God what to do? Have you ever told God what to do? We have told God what we think of the world and what we think of what is happening to us. We have told God to do something about it. So, we have told God what to do.

The "us" section of this prayer points out three daily needs: nourishment, forgiveness, and deliverance. When the first part of this prayer becomes our prayer, we get down to basics. We are able to see more readily our daily needs. We get clarity on our lives. We know what we need to survive, and we know who is the Source for what we need.

Everybody needs food daily for survival. Perhaps Jesus was especially sensitive to the needs of the day laborers whose pay at the end of the day enabled their families to eat the following day. Maybe when he referred to daily bread, he remembered his need for food during his wilderness experience. Maybe when he referred to daily bread, he recalled the history of his people in the wilderness when manna was their daily food. There was enough manna for each day, but any attempt to take more than the daily need resulted in spoilage.

We need to be reminded continually that this portion of the Learner's Prayer is an "us" section and not a "me" section. Jesus encouraged us to pray in the plural. The prayer is not, "Give me this day my daily bread." It is, "Give us this day our daily bread." I cannot pray like Jesus and pray only for myself. Concern for daily nourishment is not just concern for me and mine. Concern for daily nourishment is for all people. Carlyle Marney, pastor and founder of Interpreter's House, said what we need is for God to fix our "wanters."

There is an appropriateness in the order of things in this prayer. Abraham Maslow pointed out many years ago that there is a hierarchy of need. The Learner's Prayer expresses that. Once our physical needs for nourishment are met, there is a spiritual and emotional level of need. We need forgiveness daily so that we can be renewed spiritually and emotionally. Was Jesus saying in the Learner's Prayer that we cannot live by bread alone; that we must have forgiveness?

Sin means to do wrong, to miss the mark, the intent, or purpose of a relationship. When this happens, the relationship is ruptured and needs repair. Only forgiveness can restore the relationship. Not only do individuals sin against individuals, but we also join others in wrongdoing. The debilitating power of sin is portrayed by calling sin "debt." "This usage represents the troubled existence of an economic underclass, for which sin before God is held to be as debilitating as debt to a creditor. . . . God's transcendence is available in prayer to release us from the unbearable debt of sin."[7] Often through daily confessional prayers, we may become aware of how we have teamed up with others to do wrong. Once again it is not a "me" prayer but an "us" prayer. Forgive us.

Jesus suggested that the ability to experience forgiveness is related directly to the willingness to forgive. This is troublesome. Sometimes I want to harbor grudges or hang on to resentments. I have been wronged, and I want the one who wronged me to pay by feeling the heat of my resentment. Part of my resentment may be tied up with someone who is a repeat offender. Jesus questioned whether forgiveness had occurred if we found it necessary to keep score. Jesus said we experience forgiveness in proportion to our willingness to forgive. Daily we need to be forgiven. Daily we need to forgive.

Having asked for forgiveness, we then need deliverance. We need to be rescued from doing evil. If we have not forgiven and received forgiveness, then we are much more likely to do evil. We need forgiveness and deliverance.

The troubling parallel petition says, "Do not bring us to the time of trial, but rescue us from the evil one." Does God bring us to trials? Does God test us to determine the strength of our moral fiber? Is God some kind of heavenly psychologist who has designed the human experiment to measure how people respond to the options before them and why?

A note in the New Revised Standard Version offers another possible translation of this section: "Do not bring us into temptation." The English usage of the verb "to tempt" has a consistently negative meaning—to entice, to do wrong, to seek to seduce a person into sin, or to attempt to persuade a person to take the wrong route. If the only word we had about temptation were, "Do not bring us into temptation," then many would conclude that God does the tempting. If God does the tempting, then that at least makes God an accessory to the crime. A person cannot be held totally responsible for the crime if God enticed her or him to sin.

It is correct to hold that testing is a part of life. It is incorrect to say that testing is what God does to find out how strong or how weak we are. God knows all about us. Some have altered this testing interpretation to suggest that testing occurs so that we can know our strengths and weaknesses. However, even this interpretation turns God into a manipulator. If God sets up the testing for our education, then God is seen as maneuvering events around in our lives to try to teach us our strengths and weaknesses while running the risk of destroying us during the experiment.

Jesus' brother James later gave a clear and unprecedented statement about God not expressed elsewhere in the Bible:

> Blessed is anyone who endures temptation. Such a one has stood the test and will receive the crown of life that God has promised to those who love God. No one, when tempted, should say, "I am being tempted by God"; for God cannot be tempted by evil and God tempts no one.

> But one is tempted by one's own desire, being lured and enticed by it; then, when that desire has conceived, it gives birth to sin, and that sin, when it is fully grown, gives birth to death. (James 1:12–15)

Life is filled with temptations, and we cannot avoid them. We must determine the direction we need to move in order to be faithful and consistent in our commitment to God.

Here is the final part of the prayer: "Rescue us from the evil one." This is a prayer for salvation. To be saved means to have enough space to get away from doing evil. Is there any more urgent need or prayer or order to give God than to demand that God give us enough space to get away from doing evil? Is there anything God would rather give us than to love us enough to give us the space we need to get away from doing evil?

Deliverance from the biblical perspective is like the work of an obstetrician or midwife at the birth of a child. The midwife cannot keep the mother from experiencing pain, but she can journey with the mother in the birthing, delivery process. The possibility is very real that we will make destructive choices and decisions. We need to rely on God to guide us through those times so that when confronted with hard choices and difficult decisions, we will not give in to evil. "Do not bring us to the time of trial" is the negative way of saying, "Rescue us from the evil one." Whether stated positively or negatively, or both, one of our daily needs is to be guided away from doing evil.

A startling dimension of the Learner's Prayer is how demanding it is, giving orders to God. If perhaps, as I have suggested, Jesus suggested only a phrase at a time for his disciples to mull over and soak themselves in, then what is captured here is really a pattern for us to pray our lives. Of course, this model for us of praying our lives is based on the premise that we will have an intimate relationship with God who is portrayed as our closest friend. With the closest friend, we can be open, direct, specific, honest. That is how we need to communicate with God every day. When we do that, we will be praying like Jesus.

Anyone who has prayed the Learner's Prayer with an open heart, as an act of humble discipleship, knows that the prayer is powerful and even dangerous. To pray this prayer is to ask God to lead us down some risky and unfamiliar paths. It is to desire the realm of God to be realized on earth. To make such a request is to pledge ourselves to turn the world upside down, to reverse the social order. It is asking for a revolution. Whenever the Learner's Prayer is prayed, it is demanding and life-changing—and downright offensive.

Think about it. Consider now using the Learner's Prayer as a pattern for your own praying. Pray the Learner's Prayer, giving thought to what you are asking of God in every phrase:

Our Abba in heaven,
hallowed be your name.
Your kingdom come.
Your will be done,
on earth as it is in heaven.
Give us this day our daily bread.
And forgive us our debts,
as we also have forgiven our debtors.
And do not bring us to the time of trial,
but rescue us from the evil one. (Matt. 6:9–13)

QUESTIONS TO PONDER

1. What does the Learner's Prayer suggest to you about Jesus?
2. Why do you think the disciples asked Jesus to teach them to pray?
3. Imagine yourself to be first one and then another of the disciples. Imagine how each reacted to Jesus' instructions contained in the Learner's Prayer.
4. Pretend you have never heard the Learner's Prayer. Take some time, at least several hours but preferably several days, and soak yourself in each phrase of this prayer. Keep a journal of your thoughts, feelings, impressions, hopes, fears, dreams, and struggles as you soak yourself in each phrase.

5. Which phrase in the Learner's Prayer is most comfortable to you? Why?
6. Which phrase in the Learner's Prayer is most difficult to you? Why?
7. If the Learner's Prayer were to become your prayer, what changes in your life would you be asking God to make by praying this prayer?

CHAPTER SIX

God, Protect Them from Evil

JOHN 17:1–26

The Gospel writers mentioned many times that Jesus prayed, yet they recorded few of Jesus' actual prayers. Clearly, Jesus prayed at the time of his baptism. He also prayed in the wilderness, but we don't know exactly how he phrased those prayers. Indeed, much of his praying probably was moanings and groanings too deep for words.

The longest recorded prayer of Jesus is found in chapter 17 of John. As John arranged and presented his material, he placed this lengthy prayer of Jesus at the very end of the last meal Jesus had with his disciples just before he went to the Garden of Gethsemane.

Part of John's intent in writing his Gospel was to show that the Way, as the followers of Jesus became known, was distinct from Judaism. As John told it, the last meal Jesus had with his disciples was on the night before Passover. In John's account, the most important object lesson at the meal was Jesus' washing the disciples' feet, but no mention was made of Jesus' breaking the bread and giving the wine to his disciples.

After Jesus' efforts to cleanse the Temple, the meaning of the last meal evolved through a series of meals. During the time frame of those meals, Jesus claimed that wine and bread were a better sacrifice than what was offered in the Temple. Jesus made his meals into a rival altar. The opposition to him became deadly. Therefore, even the meal was a prayer as he declared in his last public act before his crucifixion that his meals were the center of the realm of God.[1] That was scandalous praying.

The climax of the supper segment of John's Gospel was the prayer Jesus offered for his disciples. John stressed for his readers that no follower of Jesus is ever asked to embrace the cross as depicted in chapters 18 and 19 until that person has been shown what the cross meant to Jesus, has been taught what this means for the follower, and has been prayed for by Jesus.

There is something extremely powerful about being prayed for by another person. I have noticed that when I have a prayer with someone facing surgery or recuperating from an illness or surgery, the experience is often overwhelming for the one being prayed for. Of course, several factors contribute to this overwhelming feeling. The awareness of mortality is one. In such circumstances people often are more acutely aware that the difference between life and death is one breath. I have been present when people died. It is a most unusual experience. One moment the person breathes and the next moment she doesn't. One moment she is alive and the next moment she is dead.

To be prayed for is overwhelming even when the circumstances are not life and death. Knowing that someone cares enough about me to pray for me is powerful. To pray for another with honesty and integrity is to want the very best for another. I am moved to tears knowing that someone cares deeply enough for me to want the very best for me. I also am moved to tears knowing that God wants the very best for me. For one person to address God on my behalf means that person and God are becoming partners together in wanting the very best for me. Strength and encouragement come through knowing that I am being cared for so deeply.

The converse is true. It is disturbingly troublesome when people cannot or will not bring themselves to pray for another. I have experienced people being so irritated with me that they would not pray for me. In the setting of a small group where sharing was taking place and prayers were offered by each person for the others in the group, it was painfully disturbing not to be prayed for. This discloses the intimacy of prayer, and praying for someone really does involve wanting things to go well in that person's life.

The entire seventeenth chapter of John is recorded as a prayer of Jesus. All of it is as if John put words in Jesus' mouth. It is the longest, most involved, and most intriguing prayer we have of Jesus. Jesus prayed for himself, for his disciples, and for future disciples. Some parts of the prayer are troubling because it is worded in such a way that Jesus is portrayed as moving back and forth between referring to himself in the first person and the third person. It is as if parts of the prayer are a recording of what Jesus prayed for rather than the actual prayer of Jesus. For example, if "glorify your Child so that the Child may glorify you" (v. 1) were Jesus' words, he would seem to have said, "Glorify me so that I may glorify you." Later, the wording is more in this vein: "I glorified you on earth by finishing the work that you gave me to do. So now, God, glorify me in your own presence with the glory that I had in your presence before the world existed" (vv. 4–5). John did with the prayer what Matthew did with the Learner's Prayer; he wove commentary together with the prayer.

Sometimes what we call prayers are like this. They are a mixture of our communicating with God and our making statements or announcements for others through a prayer. You've heard prayers that really were announcements for the congregation. The one praying reminds God of the various activities of the congregation and the times for the events. Authentic prayer is directed to God and invites God's involvement in the life of the one praying.

Prayer is the most intimate conversation a person can have. In the privacy of prayer, a person discloses innermost needs, feelings, and desires. Examine a person's prayers and learn exactly what that person thinks and feels about herself and about God. Jesus prayed for himself. He was astute to the circumstances around him and the emotional climate that was being expressed. He could sense that forces were closing in on him, and unless he changed his attitude and actions quickly, his life was going to end.

This prayer opens a window to the heights of God's sufficiency. With all the world shouting that Jesus was a failure, with death staring him in the face, Jesus was confident that he had done the right thing. Jesus said to God, "I glorified you on earth by finishing the work that you gave me to do" (v. 4).

What confidence! What assurance! Plenty of people faced with struggles and difficulties in life have said, "I quit." Others have shouted, "It's not fair!" Still others have commented, "If I could have just had a little more time, I could have done better." But who of us could ever say to God, "I have finished the work that you gave me to do"?

Throughout his ministry Jesus joined with people in Galilee and Judea in meals designated to anticipate the coming of the reign of God. Eating was a way of enacting the reign of God, practicing God's generosity. As a result, Jesus avoided exclusive practices that divided the people of God from one another. Suspicious characters including tax agents and others were his accepted companions. Jesus seemed always to welcome notorious sinners at the table. This approach depicted a distinct view of purity. "By moving from community to community, and having his disciples to do so, Jesus enacted his view of the generic purity of Israel. Provided one was willing to receive the forgiveness which Jesus' model of prayer referred to and his meals conveyed, the sanctity of the kingdom could be welcomed in fellowship. That was Jesus' distinctive practice of purity."[2]

Often the attitude with which one faces death reveals the depth of character and commitment one has to a principle. Jesus showed this in his words and actions as the end of his life drew near. Jesus was committed to the principle of loving the world for God's sake no matter what came to him. He refused to permit anything to dissuade him from that course of living. Even when events were the most intense, even when his closest friends betrayed and denied him, Jesus remained faithful to his relationship with God and his commitment to love God and to love other human beings as himself. There was no length to which he would not go to love people. He was a mirror of God, reflecting the love and radiance of God rather than calling attention to himself. Jesus prayed for what he could give back to God, a life of obedient service.

Thousands had stood beside him. Now, that number was reduced to a few. And even the few were going to abandon him. He could already sense that. Enough had been said and not said to let Jesus know where his disciples were emotionally. He could read their attitudes and emotions, and he could tell that as the pressure mounted, the disciples were going to cave in to the pressure. But even in sensing that, Jesus wasn't bitter toward his disciples for how he sensed they were responding. He rejoiced in what God had given him. He demonstrated that nothing can ever separate a person from the love of God by showing that nothing could cause him to stop short of sharing and showing God's love for the world. Jesus laid out a life in a way that no one had ever done. And so he could pray with confidence, "I have finished the work that you gave me to do."

Then Jesus prayed for his disciples. What a powerful event that must have been for the disciples as they listened to Jesus express his deep love, affection, and concern to God about them. First, he prayed for their protection. He wanted them to be safe. That is what salvation means, to be safe. Salvation means to have enough space to get away from doing evil. To be saved means not to be squeezed in or trapped. Paul instructed the Roman Christians, "Do not let the world squeeze you into its mold" (Rom. 12:2, author's paraphrase). Paul wanted them to have enough space for God to work with them and transform them by renewing their minds.

Peter got himself squeezed into a tight spot. Jesus wanted him to have enough space to get away from doing evil. He took Peter with him to the Garden of Gethsemane, but Peter couldn't stay awake. As I mentioned in chapter 1, maybe that contributed to Peter's being unprepared to deal with the pressures that came rapidly within a few hours. He cut off Malchus's ear. Later, he claimed he didn't have a clue who Jesus was. Then Jesus' eyes caught Peter's gaze, and how Peter wished he had taken advantage of the space available to him to keep from doing evil.

According to Luke (22:24–30), it was at this meal that the disciples got into an argument about who was the greatest among them.

Jesus tried to lead them to safety and salvation by pointing out that they were involved in a way of relating that not only went against the grain of the world but also turned the world's approach upside down. Jesus said that salvation from the envy and jealousy of greatness was in the direction of service.

At first reading, we think it was so silly and out of touch with what was happening that the disciples would spend part of their last meal with Jesus arguing about which one of them was the greatest. We tend to defend the disciples by saying they didn't know it was their last meal with Jesus. Yet if they had been paying attention at all, they would have known what jeopardy Jesus was in. They had felt the temperature rising and the pressure increasing.

"Lost" means to be in the wrong place. Judas was lost because he was in the wrong place. He got himself into a tight spot and didn't have enough room to maneuver so that he could get away from doing evil. Being in a tight spot, he was caught in the trap of betrayal. Jesus prayed that his disciples might be safe.

Even his praying for them did not keep them safe. Earlier thousands had gathered around him and hung on any crumb he offered. By the time Jesus was praying for the safety of his disciples, the thousands were reduced to a handful. Within hours the handful was down to zero. As Jesus prayed, bitterness and resentment were absent from his voice. Why? After all he had done, the efforts he had made, the clear instructions he had offered, and the warnings he had given, how could they have missed the point? How could they abandon him so quickly? There was no bitterness in Jesus' prayer because his hope was not tied up in what his disciples did or didn't do. Jesus' hope was in God. Jesus rejoiced over any evidence of the grace of God at work. Even though the disciples were scattering, emotionally and spiritually if not physically, as he was praying, Jesus saw in their gathering the work of God. A motley group they were. They had come together not because they were attracted to one another. Actually, some repelled the others. They had come together because they had been invited. They had been summoned together by a word not of their own choosing.

Jesus also prayed for the unity of his disciples. Jesus prayed that his disciples would be united in their love for the world. He wanted them to be united in their love for God and for one another in a way that reflected oneness, oneness like that his union with God reflected. Jesus was confident that people's faith would be ignited by the work of his disciples and there would be more disciples as a result of their ministry. Jesus prayed for those who would develop faith as a result of the ministry of his immediate disciples. Jesus prayed for the unity of future disciples. It is significant that unity is such a dominant theme in this prayer of Jesus. He prayed for himself and thanked God for the unity he had with God. He prayed for unity for his disciples, and he prayed for unity of future disciples. He prayed for unity but not uniformity. Jesus wanted his disciples to be united with God and one another. He was not seeking clones.

When Christian fellowship reflects in its corporate life the same kind of spiritual harmony that existed between Jesus and God, the world will realize that Jesus did not merely teach people how to be cooperative; rather, he shared with them the oneness of God. A common purpose can help hold a congregation together, but that is never enough. Even the most despotic movement can unite around a burning sense of mission. The Nazis had a common purpose. So do members of the Ku Klux Klan.

Jesus prayed that the love with which God had loved him might be in his disciples as it had been in him. The ultimate reason for a congregation to become perfectly one is a shared determination to love. Outsiders can see and recognize something unique about the union of disciples of Christ. Materials from the early centuries of the common era indicate that pagans were impressed with how Christians loved one another. If we do not, cannot, will not love other Christians, persons within the church, how will we possibly love persons outside the church?

The question to be answered is not "What do you believe?" but "How do you love?" You may have the most consistent, clear, well-developed understanding of God and people that is possible to have, but if you do not have love, it's only noise. You may have certain principles that are nonnegotiable. You may hold adamantly to those principles, but if you do not love, you accomplish nothing. You may be convinced that there is only one way to view certain issues in life and that is the right way and that is the stand you have on those issues, but if you do not love, your right view is worthless.

Jesus prayed for his disciples to be in the world but not of the world. The need for unity was essential not just that the disciples could strengthen and support one another, but that they might give visible expression to the way Jesus and God are united. That is why Jesus was praying for his disciples instead of for the world. Certainly, the world was not beyond being prayed for. However, the oneness of believers links one God and one world.

> If a band without the common ties of race or nation could stay together in a day when the world was dividing into warring camps, this would furnish tangible proof of the reconciling power of God.
>
> To shatter the solidarity of the disciple band compromises both its separation from the world and its witness to the world, for the revolutionary oneness of the church in a broken world is the best proof that what Christ has done for it was of God and not of people. In this sense, to oppose or even to weaken the unity of the church is to play the role of Judas.[3]

The values and standards of the disciples often would be in conflict with the world's standards. Jesus gave his disciples God's message of love, grace, and redemption, and the world hated them because they accepted the message and did not belong to the world. Jesus didn't say what part of the world hated the disciples. I suspect the same part that hated him, those in positions of power and popularity and prestige. Jesus was forever upsetting them because he opposed their use of the three p's—power, popularity, and prestige—for personal advantage and gain, but they were never willing to share for the benefit of others. Always persons in places of power and achievement and comfort are interested in the status quo. Jesus was interested in the status of everybody. He loved everybody and wanted everybody to have a place in the world. That was a very liberal idea, and it got him into trouble.

Later this attitude got the disciples into trouble. Jesus knew it would. That's why he prayed for them, prayed that God would protect them from evil, prayed that God would keep them safe. They needed to be kept safe so that they could carry out Jesus' liberal, liberating ministry of loving the world for God's sake.

Jesus never prayed for his disciples to be snatched out of the world or placed in a cocoon that sealed them off from the world. The world needed them involved in it if they were to be salt and light and leaven for the world. Jesus was all of those things by loving and caring for everyone. He wanted his disciples to carry on the ministry. He knew they would be tempted to withdraw from the world as the Essenes had done in seeking to be neither in the world nor of the world. Jesus also knew the disciples would be tempted to become completely absorbed in the world as the Sadducees had done. The Sadducees were both in the world and of the world. Jesus prayed for his disciples to have enough space to be safe, to be able to get away from withdrawing from the world and to get away from being absorbed in the world.

The intensity of Jesus' prayer in John 17 is somewhere between that of the Learner's Prayer and that of the Gethsemane Prayer. Clearly, it expresses Jesus' desire for his disciples, both present and future. He was praying for God's help and guidance for those who helped him. In that sense Jesus prayed for us and wants unity to be evident in our lives and relationships with God and one another. Regardless of the level of intensity, the common theme in all of Jesus' prayers is love. Whether praying for himself, for the disciples, or for future generations, always Jesus' desire was that the world be loved for God's sake.

The story is told of a man who was convicted of a crime. In prison he was a loner who had nothing to do with anyone else. The chaplain sought to befriend him, but the man rebuffed every effort of the chaplain. The prisoner made it clear verbally and nonverbally that he wanted nothing to do with the chaplain or anything the chaplain had to offer.

After some time, the chaplain died. His funeral service was held in the prison chapel. And to everyone's surprise the inmate who had consistently rebuffed the chaplain attended the funeral. A fellow inmate noticed a tear run down the man's face during the service. Afterward he approached the man and said, "Did I see you shed a tear for the chaplain? I thought you wanted nothing to do with him." The man replied, "He was the only Christ I ever knew."

That's what we are to be: Christ to one another. That's what Jesus prayed we would be when he prayed for us all to be one as he and God were one. That's what Jesus prayed when he prayed for himself to be in us and for God to be in him so the world can know that God sent him into the world and so all people can know that God loves us as God loved Jesus. Jesus prayed that we would be Christ to one another. When you pray like Jesus, you may become the only Christ some people ever know.

QUESTIONS TO PONDER

1. What meaning do you give to the movement between first and third person in the prayer of Jesus recorded in John 17?
2. What do you think it was like for the disciples to hear Jesus pray for them?
3. What is it like for you to hear someone pray specifically for you?
4. Why do we sometimes turn prayer into a bulletin board of events?
5. Compare and contrast the prayer of Jesus in John 17 with the previous prayers we have examined. What distinguishes this prayer from the others?
6. From what evil do you need to be protected?
7. What does God need to do to save you?
8. To whom might you be the only Christ that person ever knows?

CHAPTER SEVEN

Jesus' Last Wish and Testament

John 10:17–18

Seven statements are attributed to Jesus as having been spoken from the cross. The words Jesus spoke from the cross reveal the temptations he experienced in the last hours of his life and how he responded to those temptations. They are brief, pithy, one-line prayers expressing the last things about which Jesus was concerned. As he prayed his last breath, the evidence is indisputable that Jesus prayed his life and laid out his life as no one before or after him.

In tracing the praying of Jesus, we see the intimate relationship between Jesus and God. We should not be surprised that Jesus' first last word was "Abba," but we are. Perhaps it is the rapid chain of events between the "Abba" in the garden and the "Abba" from the cross that shocks us. Think of the intensity of life for Jesus during the twelve-hour period preceding his crucifixion. He had gone to supper with friends, relived the Exodus of his people, agonized in prayer, was betrayed, arrested, denied, tried, condemned, and walked up the hill to his death. With his body still aching from the scourging and the jar of dropping the cross in place, with death imminent, Jesus called out, "Abba." Jesus' relationship with God sustained him in his living and undergirded him in his dying.

The real jolt in Jesus' prayer from the cross was not "Abba," but "forgive them." Who did he want forgiven? "Them" was inclusive. Jesus must have been including the watching crowd, the scoffing rulers, the gambling soldiers, and the scattering disciples. But how could he ask forgiveness for those who turned him in, did him in, left him alone, and cheered on the executioners?

How could he pray, "Forgive them"? Perhaps because, in Gethsemane, he had prayed for himself and found resolution for the turmoil, agony, and struggle within himself, so that now he could pray, "Forgive them." But the words were shocking. They were so shocking that the early church could not endure the memory of them and dropped them. Several of the important early manuscripts did not record these words.[1] The words were too difficult for the early church. For a man being crucified to cry, "Abba, forgive them," was just too much.

Many preferred revenge to reconciliation. Some members of the church in the early years did not want Jesus forgiving Jews, Romans, Samaritans, criminals, prostitutes, or tax collectors. Some members today don't like Jesus' being so forgiving. But the church let the words stand in the best manuscripts because these words say something radically significant about Jesus and his followers.

When Jesus cried, "Abba, forgive them," he sided with people. Having sought to build a bridge to people throughout his ministry, Jesus continued his work of reconciliation even when the worst was done to him. In an early chapter of Matthew, Jesus joined people in need, adding his strength to theirs, "curing every disease and every sickness. When he saw the crowds, he had compassion for them" (Matt. 9:35–36). Later, he wept for Jerusalem. In this plea, "Abba, forgive them," he joined Jerusalem. When Jerusalem would not come to him, he went to Jerusalem. By going to Jerusalem, he stepped over the wall that separated and demonstrated how far the love of God extended. Even at the very doorway of death, Jesus expressed that love.

Why was Jesus requesting forgiveness for persons who were not seeking it themselves? When a wrong is done, the wrongdoer has separated herself from the one wronged. Strange as it seems, the quickest and healthiest forgiveness occurs when the one wronged initiates reconciliation. What a paradox! Jesus embraced those who were doing him in when he prayed, "Abba, forgive them." He offered forgiveness to people who had not repented because he saw forgiveness fueling repentance rather than repentance igniting forgiveness.

There are yet more words in this first of the last prayers of Jesus: "Abba, forgive them; for they do not know what they are doing" (Luke 23:34). Was Jesus saying that people are better off not knowing because they are unaccountable for what they do not know? God forbid! Whether the unknowing or misknowing or not knowing be circumstantial ignorance, as with the soldiers, or judicial ignorance, of which the Jews were responsible, or willful ignorance, as with us, the pathos of the situation here is that all are what Nicholas of Cusa called doctors of ignorance.[2] All of us have our Ph.D.'s in not knowing. When Jesus cried, "Abba, forgive them; for they do not know what they are doing," he expressed his desire for people to be forgiven, whatever their condition. They did not have to go to him first; he came to them. Jesus prayed for the watching crowd, the gambling soldiers, the scoffing leaders, and the scattering disciples when he said, "Abba, forgive them."

He taught his followers to pray, "Abba, forgive us our debts, as we also have forgiven our debtors" (Matt. 6:12). Jesus said to the man who was paralyzed, "Your sins are forgiven" (Matt. 9:2). The same Jesus responded to the adulteress, "Neither do I condemn you. Go your way, and from now on do not sin again" (John 8:11). And to Zacchaeus, "Hurry and come down; for I must stay at your house today" (Luke 19:5). Jesus said, "Happy are the merciful for they shall obtain mercy"; "Turn the other cheek"; "Go the second mile"; "Give your cloak and coat as well"; and "Pray for your enemies. Do good to those who hate you." Thus, the first of his last prayers gave expression to his attitude toward living and dying. He took his stand with humanity. He is living and dying proof that God is on our side.

Consider the temptations hurled at Jesus on the cross. Was he tempted to return abuse for abuse? If he could not get back at someone, could he not at least get even with somebody in the crowd or one of the thieves? He who had called and worked so hard for justice was receiving injustice. Was he tempted to scream, "Unfair!"?

There were those on whom Jesus' living and dying were not lost. One was a thief, as Luke told it. Characteristic of Luke's information about Jesus is how often he portrayed Jesus' identification with the outcasts: people with leprosy, Samaritans, adulteresses, and here, a common thief. The common thief's words seem to focus our attention on the crosses and on the cross. To view the cross in the context of the words "today you will be with me" (Luke 23:43) affects our perception of the cross.

What about Jesus' cross? Why do we focus on it? What difference is there in his cross? The other crosses made no difference. They were the instruments that the law used to break people who broke the law. *The* cross made no difference, but the *One* on the cross made the difference. The total event of Jesus' life, death, and resurrection made the difference. Who Jesus was made him the Savior and Deliverer, not what was done to him. He said, "So there will be one flock, one shepherd. For this reason God loves me, because I lay down my life in order to take it up again. No one takes it from me, but I lay it down of my own accord" (John 10:17–18). In this drama of dramas, Jesus literally died in place of Barabbas. Here we see that the battle is not for one person or for a segment of the population, but for all people everywhere. The whole human race is involved. No one is excluded.

Probably we could understand Jesus' identifying with his mother, with John or one of the other disciples who had been with him and cared about him. But what happened is difficult for us to comprehend. It really is a simple event—so simple that everyone nearly missed it. John told only that "there they crucified him, and with him two others, one on either side, with Jesus between them" (John 19:18). Matthew and Mark added a little more, but in what they added, they treated others alike. Without Luke, we would have missed something very significant.

The two thieves were brought along as a matter of expediency. If they were going to kill one person, what was it to kill a couple more at the same time? The thieves watched Jesus being crucified. They waited their turns. Their anxieties rose; terror mounted. According to Luke, one of them joined the railings, "Are you not the Messiah? Save yourself and us!" (Luke 23:39). Then a human being with a terrible reputation responded to his chance. He recognized One he had ignored. He reacted to the railing coming from his companion's cross:

"Do you not fear God?" He recognized his own guilt and cried out, "We are getting what we deserve for our deeds." He saw something new in Jesus and said, "This man has done nothing wrong." As a result of his vision, faith dawned in him, and he cried from his cross to the center cross, "Jesus, remember me when you come into your realm." Jesus went all the way to the dying criminal and made a direct promise: "Today you will be with me in Paradise" (Luke 23:40–43).

The response of the dying thief surprises us. What more hopeless person has there ever been than this criminal? He had broken the law, and he was experiencing the consequences. What chance did he have? He had no time to live a holy life. He could not learn the Learner's Prayer. He could not become a church member or be baptized or take communion. Of all the hopeless people you ever saw, this one is most hopeless. But any person, no matter how hopeless or how low, is acceptable to God. Jesus identified himself once with a person who was paralyzed, showing that those usually shunted aside might come; with a Pharisee, demonstrating that anybody could come; with a little child, clearly stating how all have to come. And Jesus identified with the thief, indicating that anyone may come. Jesus was never so wrapped in himself or so embroiled by the hurt and injustice done to him that he could not respond to the expressed need of anyone of any status. He could be a wounded healer to the one who tore away his pretension and said, "We are getting what we deserve."

These last prayers of Jesus are potent with meaning and intensity. They confirm that one person, *the Person,* died as he lived. These words tell us that the realm of God always is made up of people who feel hopeless. Each prayer from the cross we examine moves us closer to the cross. There was some comfort when we were out in the crowd, and he said, "Abba, forgive them." At least we were lost in the crowd. No names were called. When Jesus spoke to the common criminal, "Today you will be with me," we could hold that at a distance by being spectators.

But when he said, "Here is your mother" (John 19:27), Jesus got very close to home. We hear and feel the agony of family members, a mother and a son being separated. Jesus was saying to God that he wanted his mother taken care of. In communion with God and in conversation with his mother and with John he was making sure she was taken care of. We can feel the ache because we have been separated from a parent, a child, or a grandparent. The reality of the cross is stark and cold, and the ache is deep. What was it like for Mary? With life fleeing so fast, how could Jesus be conscious of who was there?

We know that Mary had a rough time of it. Life had not turned out as she had expected. On that day, all of life flashed before her. Her adolescent visions of life had been filled with joy and laughter. She and Joseph had plans and dreams and hopes. But how differently life turned out from her adolescent vision of womanhood!

In less than three years, Mary saw the utter collapse of the mission that never began to take the shape she had anticipated. She stood at the foot of the cross, dazed by stark numbness. What did she get out of it? John told us that all she got was to be a guest in John's home: "He said to his mother, 'Woman, here is your son.' Then he said to the disciple, 'Here is your mother'" (John 19:26–27). From that hour on, the disciple took her as his own.

It just isn't in the usual order of life that a mother outlive her son. Even if Mary were convinced that Jesus had done some strange things, she knew he had done nothing to deserve death, certainly not death like that. From that hour, that disciple—the only one of the apostles identified as being at the cross—took Mary as his own. But that was small comfort. Consider what she lost: in reality, a son; in her dream, a messiah who never developed as she expected. She became a hanger-on in somebody else's house. She had a place to lay her head, more than her son ever had. She was the object of the charitable love and care of one who at best was her nephew, and who might not have even been related to her, but she had expected so much more, such a different outcome.

I marvel at Jesus' consciousness and sensitivity in seeking Mary's welfare. While he was dying, Jesus was serene and calm enough to think and pray and plan for others. I can understand how Jesus would be aware of the crowd, buzzing with anticipation and shouting insults. It makes sense that Jesus would be aware of the criminals because they were beside him. I am amazed that Jesus could focus on anyone in the middle of the drama. Surely, he was in a blind haze. Was he not tempted to think only of himself and feel only his pain? He saw his mother, and the fact that he saw her is like a precious kiss. It seems like such a small incident, but how much of human life passes in little incidents!

We are up close to the cross and we feel uncomfortable. As we come closer to the cross, as we see how this One died like he lived, the words of A. J. Gossip are an inspiration. With respect to his own death he said,

> God grant that when the dark is falling round us in that last scene of all, when the poorest of us, for once, hold the center of the stage, may we face death with a like unselfishness—not fidgeting about ourselves, not hurriedly making last-minute preparations, but packed and ready and waiting for the tide, may we be able eagerly to enter into the happiness and interest of those around us . . . that for us, too, death may be no squalid thing, but big and . . . invincible.[3]

The whole world watched and watches Jesus die. No person ever died in the presence of so many watchers. He died for and in view of the whole world; and yet in the moment of his dying for the whole world, he reached out to identify with his mother. We have watched him all along his journey, but nowhere was he more human than when he said, "Here is your mother." And nowhere in the journey was he more completely worthy, from the human side, of being called the Child of God.

Does reading this affect you as it does me while I am writing it? I feel drained. I feel as if I'm in a marathon here. These prayers from the cross express an intense, emotionally charged event. This is emotionally exhausting. I'm not sure I can go on. My mouth feels dry. I need a drink.

Jesus' next prayer was, "I am thirsty" (John 19:28). We have in this prayer of Jesus no postoperative thirst, no playacting from a desert scene. There was a real human being who had all of life wrung out of him. Through the agonizing experience of crucifixion, he tended to the needs of the crowd, "Abba, forgive them," the needs of a common thief, "Today you will be with me," and the needs of his mother, "Here is your son. . . . Here is your mother." To pray life like that is for one to have life drained from him.

Jesus' reason for saying he was thirsty, according to John, was to fulfill Scripture. Jesus quoted a portion of Psalm 69. No doubt Jesus and John were familiar with the psalm, written as personal and community expression by people worshiping God. Jesus and others read his situation in life and quoted these words as a means of expressing what was occurring. We often quote Tennyson, Shakespeare, and others to illustrate and communicate our feelings and experiences. It was natural for the earlier followers of Jesus to find in their hymnal, the Psalms, words that Jesus himself had quoted, and they used them to describe their teacher.

Who of us has not found a portion of one of the Psalms that described our situation? When we make such a discovery, that passage becomes implanted in our lives. We have done for ourselves what Jesus did. In his agony and praying Jesus quoted from a psalm what he felt and needed, "I am thirsty."

Jesus was thirsty, and even that basic need was a temptation to him. The battle inside was between underexpression and overexpression. Was he tempted to deny his thirst with the claim that "real men don't get thirsty"? Was he tempted to make a scene and draw the attention of all people to himself by shouting out how terrible his thirst was? Once again, he walked the straight and narrow path between the options, admitting he was a human being with a basic human need—"I am thirsty."

There seemed to be a double identifying. He was identifying with the thirst of all Israel and with a basic human need. All Israel thirsted for, longed for, the Messiah, God's deliverer. As Moses had brought the children of Israel out of the parched land of Egypt, every Israelite hoped that the Messiah would come to the dry and thirsty land of Israel and bring a spring of living water that never would run dry.

With his cry, "I am thirsty," Jesus expressed a basic human need.

Water is our most basic need. Without water, a person might exist three days. Isn't it amazing how just a small drink can soothe and comfort? As surgical patients begin to return from the land of the unconscious, a few ice chips can bring great refreshment and comfort, if only briefly. When a person is near death, about the last thing she can be is thirsty. Even when people can't eat, they can still drink. About the last power a person has is to drink.

The theme of thirst is a thread running through the ministry of Jesus: "Blessed are those who hunger and thirst for righteousness, for they will be filled" (Matt. 5:6). One of the early events in his ministry, if not the first event, was Jesus' encounter with a Samaritan woman at a well in Sychar. In essence, Jesus said to her, "I'm thirsty." His words were, "Give me a drink" (John 4:7). The conversation expanded from that point, and Jesus spoke about an eternal thirst-quenching source of living water. Jesus claimed to offer the kind of refreshing water that would become a spring of life-giving water within the person. Jesus, who was thirsty, asked for a drink. Then he promised a gift by which one would never be thirsty again. Yet as his life ended, nearly his last prayer was asking for a drink, "I am thirsty."

John recorded that Jesus needed a drink and that Jesus drank the wine, a cheap wine such as was a common drink of Roman soldiers. This prayer of Jesus, "I am thirsty," is another difficult word for the church. The earlier Gospels don't have it. For Jesus to be thirsty makes him too human, more human than many are willing to permit. But this is identification with us. On the cross, Jesus had run to the end of this human track. He had come all the way. With a taste of wine to wet his parched mouth, he came to the end of human ability and resources, and he stood completely identified with us. From John's perspective, Jesus' ministry opened and closed with the same words, "I am thirsty."

Can you imagine what this prayer about his thirst must have done to Mary? That might have been the worst cry of all to bear. To hear one of my children cry out in the darkness, "I'm thirsty," and to be unable to give her a cup of water would be horrid. Much earlier Jesus had said that whoever gave a cup of cold water to anyone in his name served the realm of God. Do you suppose that Jesus had any way of knowing that someday a lad, a Roman soldier, or a young Jew would run and get something for him to wet his thirst? Someone, unnamed, unknown, soaked a sponge in wine and lifted it to Jesus' lips, and he drank.

Jesus made a sacrament out of every glass of water. He makes a priest out of every stumbling, faltering, fumbling person who moves from a faucet to the person who says, "I'm thirsty." We need to remember what it is to thirst. Every time we take a drink of water, we ought to remember the sacrament of thirst.

Great moments and opportunities come like all other moments and opportunities, and the greatness comes in how we handle the events. From the experience of Jesus we can conclude correctly that whoever lifted a wine-soaked sponge to Jesus' lips was kind to him. When Jesus was in the process of dying, the unknown person did something to help Jesus through the parched land. There is no need for envy and wishing we could do something as worthwhile just once in our lives. All of us have the same opportunities. Jesus always was touched by people's needs and infirmities, and thus, he accounted anything done to aid the most insignificant as done to him.

There are no easy final words. It is never easy to speak a final word or hear a final word. The last prayers of Jesus are difficult, but perhaps none is as difficult as this: "My God, my God, why have you forsaken me?" (Mark 15:34). What was he saying? What did he mean? How are we to understand him? We want to turn loose of this prayer long before it turns loose of us.

Was Jesus tempted to curse God and die? He expected the enterprise of being God in the flesh to be filled with risks and difficulties, but did he know it would come to such a situation? The pain was more intense than he had anticipated. The verbal and physical spit were degrading. How could God have gotten Jesus into such dire straits? "My God, my God, why have you forsaken me?" may be the ultimate prayer of Jesus.

Would God abandon God's own Child? Why? Jesus earlier had promised he would never abandon his followers. For what reason would God abandon Jesus? If God did abandon Jesus, does that mean there may come some tough times in our lives when God cannot stay with us? There had been other agonizing cries to God. Only a few hours earlier Jesus had said, "God, if it is possible, let this cup pass from me." From the cross he had prayed, "Abba, forgive them." In another moment we will hear Christ pray, "Abba, into your hands I commend my spirit." God heard the first prayer and the other prayers. The cries do not suggest the three traditional explanations of delirium, desolation, or dereliction. Quite the contrary, prayers such as "My God, my God . . ." demonstrate a most intimate, honest relationship with God. Many believe that God abandoned Jesus and that this prayer of Jesus depicts the depth of his despair. Martin Dibelius, a scholar of the Christian Scriptures, offers another point of view by saying that one does not quote Scripture in prayer when he has given up his faith.[4] George Buttrick reports in a sermon that there hangs in a chapel in Milan an early Renaissance painting of the crucifixion in which, late in the evening, when the light allows it and when viewed from a certain angle, a shadowy figure seems to have been interposed between Christ and the wood of the cross.[5] The artist was saying God was there too.

Ernst Käsemann insists that this cry be understood as evidence that Jesus died like he lived.[6] Jesus died with God's word on his lips and with unshaken trust in God who alone and always is one's true help. If God's back was turned on Jesus, we are saying that there are some difficult times in life when we may expect God to check out on us if life becomes too strenuous. This makes faith in God rather precarious, causing us to wonder if our present situation is the one when God's support will be withdrawn. The promise of God is always to be with us. That was a promise by which Jesus lived and died. Jesus lived out a life the way a life is to be lived. He invites us to do the same, and the source of help and hope to live as Jesus did is God, who never abandons people solely to their own resources.

Jesus, feeling the loneliness and abandonment of his companions, told us what it is like to be utterly human, left solely to our own resources. Jesus' prayer, "My God, my God . . . ," is an expression of loneliness and perplexity over the betrayal, the desertion, and the cross. As much as is possible for God to dwell in a human being, God dwelt in Jesus. In essence the Jewish leaders, the Roman soldiers, and the crowd had God in their hands. The cross displays what people do when they have God in their hands.

"Abandonment" was and is a difficult word. Some thought Jesus was calling for Elijah. According to the Hebrew Scriptures, Elijah transcended death, and legend had it that he came to the aid of persons in great distress. I do not know if any true Jew could have heard Jesus say "Eloi" and mistaken it for "Elijah." People can hear almost anything they wish to hear. Those who heard his cry knew him. Those who had no wish to hear, those who had no hope of hearing, heard him call Elijah, and ran to substitute vinegar. They offered him cheap wine similar to vinegar, probably in an attempt to deaden the pain, because they thought he was delirious from physical pain. But the emotional pain of abandonment by family or friends cannot be lessened with painkillers. Jesus knew that, and his prayer verbalized the deep agony he felt because of the desertion of those in whom he had invested so much of himself.

As Jesus looked in disbelief into the absence of his friends, he was tempted to say nothing. At that late hour, what good would more words be? Three years of talking had brought him to a cross where his friends would not show their faces. Jesus might have been tempted to say too much, to lash out in verbal abuse at his absent supporters or at those who turned him in and did him in. Rather, he chose a third alternative. He called out to his absent friends to give an account of themselves, and he cried out to God. His prayer resisted the shortcut of saying nothing or saying too much, and it penetrated to the essence of his disciples' actions and God's help.

Jesus was suspended between heaven and earth on two pieces of wood. To whom was he looking when in anguish he uttered, "My God, my God, why have you forsaken me?" I submit he was looking to God and looking at the crowd. He was looking to God with confidence and assurance of God's constant abiding presence that Psalm 22 affirms. I submit he was looking at the crowd, at us, and praying in agony to God for help and strength because they/we abandoned him when he most needed the love and support of friends. We are scared and scattered, hiding, seeking asylum somewhere, anywhere. Cutting through the darkness of noonday is this stark, agonizing prayer: "My God, my God, why have you forsaken me?"

So little in life is ever finished. We touch the high spots hurriedly. The sand in the hourglass runs out. We must stop. The ball game may be over. The exam may have been taken. The funeral service may have been conducted. We may summarize by saying, "It is past." But who of us can say that anything is ever finished?

Having listened to the taunts of the crowd and feeling the abandonment of friends, was Jesus tempted to conclude his life had been a waste? Did he want to resign from life and get it over? Even at the very end of life, Jesus' prayer expressed his resistance to giving in to the easy, quick solution.

The Gospels reported differently the last breath of Jesus. Matthew and Mark noted that he gave a loud cry and died. Luke reported that he cried out in a loud voice, "Abba, into your hands I commend my spirit" (Luke 23:46), and died. John wrote that Jesus said, "It is finished," bowed his head, and died (John 19:30). The last prayer of Jesus reverberated against the stark silence of those who watched. What does it say to us who stand uncomfortably, first on one foot and then on the other, and watch? Jesus did not die by some decree of God's will to buy off Satan. He did not die to satisfy a pagan god of legal righteousness, to ransom a kidnapped person, or to keep us from having to die. Jesus was at the end of the track, where he could no longer see anything, and by an act of faith he turned the outcome over to God. It was not as if Jesus went his whole life without praying, without calling on God, and then called on God when time was gone. It was not as if God had never before heard his voice. Here is the last picture of an unshaken faith agonizing its way to breathe its last, when the final surge of pain is over.

John recorded the last prayer of Jesus: "It is finished." Hope was gone, or so it seemed. Everything for which Jesus had toiled and sacrificed seemed gone, lost, and soon to be forgotten. Maybe Calvary did mean that Jesus and his kind always would be so wide of the mark, so absolutely beside the point, that they were bound to come out all through the ages at the little end of everything and be wiped clean off the slate at last. After all, nothing had come of all that Jesus had taught and planned and done and suffered, except for a little group who claimed to love and a scattered group who had believed in him for a while and then fled.

Luke's account of the last prayers of Jesus opened and closed with the same address, "Abba." Luke began with "Abba, forgive them," and concluded with "Abba, into your hands . . ." The intimate, loving relationship with God as Parent that began early in Jesus' life, which nurtured him in his growth, his struggles, and his living, also sustained him in his dying. Here we are only three hours later in the life of Christ than when we began this chapter. But with what intensity Jesus lived those three hours! Once again, with Jesus being supremely human, he experienced the truth of another's words as expressive of his confidence. "Abba, into your hands . . ." is a quote from Psalm 31.

This prayer by Jesus reveals an unashamed commitment of trust fully discharged. There may not be many who are conscious of any sense of completion when death comes to them. There was every reason for Jesus to have had a sense of incompletion. He was cut off at the threshold of life. No accusation could be supported against him. He was kind. The most pathetic commentary on human life is the list of his enemies. Here we see him coming to an untimely death as he was turning into manhood, his ministry just budding, barely in the spring of its development. The possibilities were unfathomed and the hopes were unrealized. Wherever he had gone around the countryside, trouble had followed. Jesus could not even die in a solitary state, for two thieves were crucified with him. The ones he had attempted to teach had betrayed, denied, and fled. Those who were closest to him in living were at a distance in his dying, saying, "We never thought it would come to this." Even with all of this, Jesus could pray, "Abba, into your hands . . ."

This prayer of Jesus was not sad resignation, as the medieval artists tended to portray. Although the biblical accounts noted that he stumbled as he walked toward Golgotha, there was no indication anywhere that stumbling was caused by uncertainty. Actually, the opposite seemed evident. The whole day with all its tragedy and horror and awfulness seemed pervaded by a sense of untroubled certainty.

There were numerous examples of uncertainty, but not in Jesus. There was no certainty in Pilate. He came in, went out, sat down, stood up, gave judgments, went back on them, excused himself by allowing others to decide for him, washed his hands. There was no certainty in the frantic mob. Their vacillation was depicted in their cheers, "Hosanna!" one day and "Crucify!" the next. No certainty was seen in the frightened disciples. Peter spoke with the greatest commitment and acted with the least. The disciples observed the crucifixion from a distance. The Sanhedrin expressed no certainty. They were disorganized and confused. Some members, but not all, were certain that if they could be rid of Jesus, their troubles would end.

Only Jesus seemed deliberate, masterful, certain. Each step he chose. He refused the drug. The accusers, the crowd, and the executioners were forgiven. A thief was made the object of a grand promise. A sorrowing mother was given over to the tender hands of a disciple.

Following twenty-four hours of agony, taunting misery, trial, and crucifixion, Jesus said, "It is finished." But his statement was not about twenty-four hours of life; it was about thirty-three years of living. How life is to be lived was lived out by him. As a human being, he could lay out a life as God intended a life to be laid out. Indeed, Jesus could and did pray his life. Jesus could finish.

In contrast, John Ruskin's comments about art are descriptive of our attempts at finishing:

> Our best finishing is but coarse and blundering work after all. We may smooth and soften and sharpen till we are sick at heart; but take a good magnifying glass to our miracle of skill, and the invisible edge is a jagged saw, and the silky thread a rugged cable and the soft surface a granite desert. . . . God alone can finish; and the more intelligent the human

> mind becomes, the more infiniteness of interval is felt between human and divine work in this respect.[7]

What can the best of us take back to God? Some broken promises? A few attempts that came to little? Maybe some dreams that went out, or that came true and proved most disappointing? We use our brief span of life learning how to live; and having learned a little, we get no chance to put it into practice. We often conclude that because a segment of life has ended, we have done our best. That is relief. Jesus enabled people to know God and to know humanity and life as they are created by God to be. Jesus expressed certainty in knowing that he had carried through completely and his work was finished.

Was the temptation there for Jesus to beg for more time, another minute, another hour? Having taken the long way around all along, perhaps it was not so difficult to do the same at the end. He examined the life that he had laid out. He had finished. That is a final prayer. It stirs us because we are so far away from finishing anything, especially laying out our lives as God intended lives to be lived. Jesus' last wish and testament was to lay down his life for his friends. In an effort to do that Jesus prayed his life. As death came to him, Jesus turned up an empty cup. Death took nothing from Jesus because he had poured out all the contents of his life. He prayed his last prayer, "It is finished. Into your hands I commend my spirit," and breathed his last breath.

QUESTIONS TO PONDER

1. Which of Jesus' prayers from the cross is most comforting to you? Why?
2. Which of Jesus' prayers from the cross is most disturbing to you? Why?
3. Why do you think that Jesus was able to pray as he did from the cross?
4. What needs to happen in your life in order for you to be able to pray like Jesus did from the cross?

CHAPTER EIGHT

Praying for Yourself

LUKE 11:1

Do you remember anything about the first instructions you were given about prayer? Having examined some of the prayers recorded in the Bible, I can tell you that no one ever suggested that I pray like what I discover there. Jeremiah's approach to God is not the way I learned to pray for myself:

> *Cursed be the day on which I was born!*
> *The day when my mother bore me,*
> *let it not be blessed!*
> *Cursed be the man*
> *who brought the news to my father, saying,*
> *"A child is born to you, a son,"*
> *making him very glad. (Jer. 20:14–15)*

Consider the Psalms. Harold Kushner suggests that the Psalms is God's favorite book because it tells what people think about God. Have you ever had some of these thoughts about God?

> *Rouse yourself! Why do you sleep, O God?*
> *Awake, do not cast us off forever!*
> *Why do you hide your face?*
> *Why do you forget our affliction and oppression? (Ps. 44:23–24)*

In teaching people to love God and human beings, Jesus underscored the necessity for people to love themselves. That principle applies in our praying too. We must pray for ourselves. We will not pray any more earnestly or openly for others than we pray for ourselves. Jesus prayed for himself, and we must pray for ourselves.

Jesus' disciples asked, "How do we learn to pray?" Jesus answered, "Pray." He offered the Learner's Prayer discussed in chapter 5 as an illustration and model. Praying like Jesus means we request Christ to teach us to pray just as the first followers of Christ requested, "Teach us to pray, as John taught his disciples" (Luke 11:1).

Prayer is the communication system between people and God. On a personal and individual level, prayer is communication between friends. On first meeting, two people often appear aloof to each other. A friendship does not develop by each nodding to the other occasionally. As they experience mutual events and share joys and sorrows, empathy develops; bonding occurs. A friendship is established that can last a lifetime. So it is with friendship beyond time. Prayer is the communication system of this friendship. Prayer becomes an experience of love and trust leading to self-disclosure; as a result, I discover myself to be at one with God. Sarah Breathnach expresses this idea in her daily devotional material:

> In its purest form, prayer is conversation. Communion. Connection. Intimacy. Prayer is the dialect of Divinity. Prayer is actually the authentic conversation because you don't have to hold back; you can say whatever needs to be said, exactly the way you want to express it, when you want to express it. You won't be judged. You won't risk losing love; instead, by praying you will increase your awareness of it. You won't have to phrase your words carefully lest there be misunderstandings, because you can't be misunderstood.[1]

I feel in conflict with God when I perceive my words and actions have not communicated love, justice, and mercy. Attempting to put myself in God's place is helpful in praying. Such an approach enables me to tell God anything because I admit that God already knows it. I feel at one with God when I express my joys and agonies and feel that God has listened, that what is happening to me matters to God.

These expressions may take no verbal forms but be groanings directed toward God.

Thus, words are not essential for this oneness to occur. On October 3, 1972, I stood in a hospital corridor gazing through a glass into a face I had never seen before. My prayer took the shape of tears rolling down my cheeks. There was Melanie. No words could say what I felt. My tears thanked God for the gift of life in the form of a daughter.

We are relational creatures by nature and by need. As created beings, we have the capacity to relate to other human beings and to God. But we erect barriers that block our communing with God. As Jesus suggested in the parable of the prodigal son, we are not our authentic selves apart from God. When we are apart from God, we are in a crisis. No matter what our efforts, we feel out of touch with God, and every attempt to communicate with God fails. Attempts to pray become meaningless. When this happens to me, I feel I am in the far country and my communing with God is blocked. Barriers in my relating with God include low self-esteem, anger, fear, and guilt.

When I was a teenager, I suffered from a superiority complex. Others saw me as self-assured, even conceited. Actually, I was shaky and frightened. I overcompensated for inferior feelings by acting superior. I did not consider myself worth much and doubted that anyone would like me. Thomas Merton once said that there is only one thing a person desires more than happiness and that is approval. I had an insatiable appetite for approval, which I thought would say I was somebody. It was natural for me to transfer my perceptions about authority figures and their expectations onto God, the ultimate authority figure. I concluded there must be a routine or ritual I could do that would please God and gain God's approval.

Where I grew up, the beatitude of reality was, "Blessed are they who work hard, for they shall earn acceptance and approval." I wrapped myself in doing because I saw the acceptance and approval of God determined by visible, measurable, tangible accomplishments just as grades given in school measured my comprehension of a subject. Prayer at that juncture was static monologue: "Sovereign

God, tell me what you want me to do." When I listened for a response, all I perceived was, "Don't do anything that anybody won't like!" Why bother? Prayer became meaningless. I continued my perfunctory religious rituals, including saying prayers. Reflecting on that time, I realize that saying prayers is revealing. I was not praying. I was saying prayers. Since then I have discovered there are times when I can say the prayers of others and I am genuinely praying. I also may say my prayers and discover my heart is not in them. At those times the form may be prayer, but the content is not.

I was helped over the low self-esteem barrier to prayer when someone suggested that Jesus said we had to love ourselves in order to love others. My concept of prayer began to change as I discovered there was a correlation between my love for God, my love for others, and my feelings about myself. As I began to discover I was a person of worth, created by God, I realized what happens to me matters to God. What liberation! What healing! I can tell God how I feel without fear of reprisal or rejection. Here is an example:

> God,
>
> I don't want to be here today. I have every reason to like it here, but the pit of my stomach is a churning bundle of anxiety. All the outward signs point toward happiness and success. Have I become secure in this place? Is it now time to move to another place? Or am I really insecure here and hope to find security somewhere else?
>
> What shall I do? I'm unhappy but I don't know why. My motivation is gone. I don't want to work here anymore. Amen.

Feelings of low self-esteem continue to surface periodically. When they do, the prayer barrier goes up. Failure to express my feelings of low esteem results in prayer reverting to a meaningless static monologue.

Anger often blocks prayer. My early learning equated anger with sin. I still remember the relief I felt the day I stumbled over Ephesians 4:26–27, "Be angry but do not sin; do not let the sun go down on your anger, and do not make room for the devil." Anger is a feeling—

it is neither right nor wrong. Anger is part of my natural warning system that helps me identify a potential problem. I need to get at the root of the problem and seek to dissolve my anger appropriately.

A woman who was angry at God because life had not gone well for her said to her son, who was anticipating surgery, "I would pray for you if I believed in prayer anymore." She believed God should have worked out things better for her. She was angry at her circumstances and ultimately angry at God, and the barrier kept her from consciously communicating with God. Her prayer crisis was caused by the barrier of anger.

Job took a different approach. Job expressed his anger to God several times. Here is one example:

As for me, is my complaint addressed to mortals?
Why should I not be impatient?
Look at me, and be appalled,
and lay your hand upon your mouth.
When I think of it I am dismayed,
and shuddering seizes my flesh. (Job 21:4–6)

Job discovered that God was big enough to receive his anger and not destroy him. Making this discovery for myself has aided me in dealing constructively with the strong emotion of anger. I need to tell God my feelings even though I know God knows what they are. If I am detained because my wife is late, I become angry. She knows I am angry and why. I know I am angry and why. The wall of tension, however, continues to separate us until we verbalize our feelings to each other and dissolve the anger. The same is true when I am angry at God. My telling God my feelings is part of the process necessary to tear down this barrier to prayer.

Intimacy with God involves self-disclosure, and that is threatening! Fear often blocks my communication with God. My fear of rejection by God keeps me from stating my innermost thoughts and desires. Fear controls me in spite of my intellectual awareness that God already knows my thoughts and feelings. How could God possibly love me if I told God what I really think? is the bottom line of my fear.

Jacob's fear controlled him. For twenty years Jacob ran scared. Although he said his prayers during those twenty years, he was not really one with God until that episode by the Jabbok River when he wrestled all night long. Realizing that he could no longer hide, he named his fears to himself and to God. The wall came down, Jacob passed through one of his prayer crises, and his whole identity was changed.

If it isn't low self-esteem, anger, or fear blocking my communication with God, then it is guilt. The emotional reaction to having done something wrong is guilt. Guilt does its damage because the guilty person tries to deal with guilt alone, which is about as easy as sitting on one's own lap.

The biblical word for wrongdoing is "sin." Although sin may be against another person, it always is against God. When we sin, we feel guilt. Guilt is a barrier to prayer. It causes us to feel separated from God and unable to be our true selves until we invite God to deal with our guilt.

Guilt blocked communication with God for Judas, who attempted to deal with his guilt alone. He sought relief from his guilt by returning the money he had received. When that did not work, Judas was overcome with despair, becoming so confused that he was blind to any presence other than his own. Judas saw no solution other than his own and conceived of no absolution beyond himself. Judas had himself on his hands. He tied the rope around his neck and kicked away the stool, trying alone to get himself off his hands. Guilt was a barrier to prayer for Judas.

There are other barriers to prayer for me. They may occur separately or in a variety of combinations. They declare prayer null and void and create a prayer crisis. With God's help in identifying these barriers, they can come down, and we can commune with God as friend with friend. This is prayer.

The most important thing Jesus said about prayer is to keep at it. Doing that requires discipline. A cursory reading of Luke 11:1–13, as well as the parable of the unjust judge, has led to the assumption that if we pester and badger God long enough, God eventually will give us what we want. Ask, search, and knock have been interpreted too often as God's saying, "Your wish is my command." Such a description of God makes God a heavenly bellhop at our disposal. Persistent praying is not wringing gifts from an unwilling God. Persistence in prayer is an act of faith. It is a testimony to our belief in a loving, personal God. We are going to One who knows our needs better than we know them ourselves and whose attitude toward us is one of generous love.

I am confident that God answers every prayer, and I do not mean with a trite yes, no, maybe, or later. Rather, God answers every prayer by listening. That is a response. Frustration springs up in me when I am in a conversation with a person and I see her eyes wander. What has distracted her? Is she disinterested in me? Is she bored with what I am saying? I know she isn't listening. I may stop talking and she doesn't even notice! Jesus said this will never happen with prayer. "When you pray," he said, "ask [and you will receive a hearing], search [and you will find a listening Friend], knock [and the door of receptiveness will be opened to you]."

As a pastor, I have had to keep at prayer. My interest and need for prayer have caused me to reflect on my prayer pilgrimage, which indicates how praying has evolved for me. My prayer pilgrimage discloses a changing view of God. Perhaps your journey is similar to mine.

My earliest visual image of God was that of a grand, old, white-bearded man. Although he did not wear a red suit or have a cottony beard, the similarity to Santa Claus is evident. The similarity was reflected not only in my visual image but also in the words of my prayers. Long after my belief in Santa Claus had changed, my concept of God continued to be tainted by Santa. My early prayers were filled with magic and fantasy. Somewhere, probably at church and at home, I had learned that I should just ask God for whatever I wanted because he (at that time my only concept of God was masculine) could do anything. I wanted a train set, and the substance of my prayers was, "God, I want a new electric train." After several days passed and God did not deliver, I prayed, "God, *please* give me a new electric train." Still, no train. I suggested, "God, since you can do anything, why don't you just make me a train? If you make it, it won't be like any other train anybody has ever seen." What an opportunity for God! Here was God's chance to prove to me and everyone I knew what a great train builder God could be. Much later I did receive an electric train, but I didn't think God had anything to do with my receiving it. Sometime earlier I had concluded that God wasn't into giving trains to kids.

As I grew in stature and wisdom, I also grew in fear of God. It was *real* fear. There was no awe in it. I began to perceive that God was demanding a "pound of flesh." If God could do anything, destroying me was in the realm of possibilities, and I was afraid God would destroy me. I was a sinner in the hands of an angry God. What must I do? God seemed so angry that I doubted I had the capacity to make God happy, but I hoped I could make God not be angry, neutralize God. I began to work my "magic" ritual to combat God's anger. I developed a compulsion to pray every day, usually lying in bed in the darkness of the night before I dozed off to sleep. On several occasions, I awoke with the jolt of awareness that I had forgotten to "say my prayers." I was glad God had let me live but more frightened than ever, thinking I had made God angrier at me. The content of those prayers, as I recall, was evidence that I was saying prayers rather than praying: "God, please forgive me for forgetting to pray today. Help me to be a better person. Forgive me for all the sins I have committed today, even the ones I didn't know I did. Amen." Such phrases now seem like a version of "Now I lay me down to sleep . . . should I die before I wake, I pray God my soul to take."

About that time in my life, I began playing sports. As I did, I was concerned that God be on my side, passing out favors in the form of victories. Only much later did it occur to me to wonder if I were on God's side. Now, I know God always is on my side and on the side of everyone else. Being on my side does not exclude God from being on the side of another. Life is not made up of winners and losers from God's perspective.

I prayed for getting hits in baseball and making free throws in basketball. Interestingly enough, I did not pray to avoid errors in baseball or to make field goals in basketball. The action was too intense to think about praying at those times. I prayed for my team to win and arrogantly assumed God would reward me because I prayed, read the Bible, and went to church. God was indebted to me; God owed me some favors. I never considered there might be someone on the other team doing exactly what I was doing. I did discover that often the other's athletic performance was better than mine, and I discovered that made the difference in winning and losing sports events. Who won ball games was not God's concern.

When I went to college, my view of God changed from that of being a favor giver to being a distant, aloof creature. God knew all that I did as well as my every thought. Since God already knew all, I saw no reason to spend energy communicating my needs to God. Jesus had said that God knew my needs even before I did, so why bother? Although God was distant, I would never have said that God was absent. I thought God was still at my bidding to snatch me out of threatening situations. God also was convenient to fill in the gaps in my comprehension of life. Whatever I could not explain, I said, "God did it."

My thinking processes expanded in many areas, but when it came to understanding what God was like, I kept God as small as possible. There was a secure feeling in knowing how God functioned and where God fit in the scheme of things. Then I enrolled in a survey course of the Hebrew Scriptures. I can still feel the agony of those first six weeks of class. I can see myself walking around the campus in a daze. The professor gently, firmly encouraged me to take the Bible seriously. Flexibility might have characterized my approach toward learning in other areas, but when it came to the Bible and God, rigidity was my security.

Some of my more meaningful praying occurred during those six weeks, although I did not call it praying at the time. I was in agony, conflict, struggle too deep for words, but the Spirit was pleading my case with God. Everything seemed to be up for review and reconsideration in my life: my vocational choice, my marital choice, my view of God, my view of the world, and my view of myself. I had put God in a box and was planning on keeping God right there for the rest of my life. I had determined how God would function. I was wrestling with the God in whom I had believed. Out of the fuzziness of all of this struggle came a glimmer of light in the form of a question: If God were what I claimed God to be, namely, God, and if God could do all I said I believed that God could do, namely, create the universe and other universes, then why was I setting limits on how and when all of this was done? In struggling with my view of God, I was struggling with my concept of prayer and vice versa. God was my Contender.

I began asking, What is God like? The answer for me was in Jesus. As I searched the Gospels, I saw a compassionate Friend rather than the Contender of earlier days. Suddenly, the Exodus statement about God speaking to Moses as a Friend (33:11) leaped off the page. Certainly, God is beyond us, greater than and more than we ever can comprehend. Yet God also is present with us and to us as a Friend of the highest order. Jesus portrayed God as a loving, intimate Friend. The more my view of God is one of a compassionate Friend, the better able I am to commune with God. The more like Santa Claus, Angry Old Man, Favor Giver, Gap Filler, or Contender I perceive God to be, the more distance I want in this relationship and the less able I am to communicate with God. With an intimate friend I will share anything and everything. God, as revealed in Jesus, is an intimate Friend par excellence.

A significant development in my personal growth has occurred as a result of my struggle with prayer. As my view of God has moved toward knowing God as an intimate Friend, the meaning and value of prayer have increased, and my view of myself has improved. There is a direct correlation between what God is like, the significance of prayer, and self-esteem.

As I have sought to pray for myself, the Learner's Prayer has been a helpful model for me. Through it I have recognized three of my daily needs: food, forgiveness, and deliverance. Awareness of these daily needs and God's desire to meet these needs has positively affected my daily communion with God. Here is a prayer I voiced recently regarding my need for food:

> God,
>
> The scales tell me what you've been telling me for a long time. Daily I consume more than I need. I have this "wanting" compulsion. Help me to know that daily you will provide what I need but not what I want. Slowly, I am realizing that when I take more than I need, I am taking from someone else. I need your help in fixing my "wanters" so that I may experience the miracle of your sufficiency fully and become part of the solution to the daily needs of others, rather than part of the problem as I have been in the past. Amen.

Once our physical needs are met, we may turn our attention to our spiritual and emotional well-being. We need the daily renewal that comes through forgiveness of sins. Was not Jesus saying in the Learner's Prayer that a person cannot live by bread alone? One must have forgiveness.

Sin means to do wrong, to be concerned only for myself with no consideration for the needs of others. Sin is craziness. Jesus said the prodigal came to his senses when he planned to confess, "Father, I have sinned against heaven and before you; I am no longer worthy to be called your son; treat me like one of your hired hands" (Luke 15:18–19). God is the One who can deal properly with our sins, and daily we need to confess our sins to God. Here is one of my recent confessional prayers:

> O God,
>
> Sin scorches my life and makes it barren. I know that your forgiveness is the only oasis for my parched life. Hear my confession.
>
> I have done wrong and blamed it on another. Forgive me.
>
> I have benefited from the hurt of another and enjoyed it. Forgive me.
>
> I have passed on information that was confidential. Forgive me.
>
> I have refused to look into the eyes of the hungry. Forgive me.

I have resisted taking the hand of the lonely. Forgive me.
I have refused to touch the sick. Forgive me.
I have avoided the bereaved and dying. Forgive me.
Cleanse me, God. Make me whole again so that I may live—live for you. Amen.

We have sinned as individuals, and we have joined others in wrongdoing. Through daily confessional prayers, we may become aware of how we have teamed up with others to do wrong. Is this what Jesus had in mind when he suggested that his disciples pray, "Forgive us . . ."? Our collective sins include overconsumption, prejudice, and revenge, to name only three. Daily we need to come to our senses by confessing our collective sins.

Dear God,

We have contaminated our lives with sins and stunted the growth you offered us. We confess our sins to you. Hear our pleas. Forgive us for our sins as we forgive those who sin against us.

We have not just disagreed with one another. We have been mean and vindictive in our attitudes toward others. Forgive us for our mean-spiritedness and our vindictiveness.

We have been so determined to take care of ourselves that we have taken from others. Forgive us for our greed.

We have looked at and listened to others. When their skin color and accent were different from ours, we put them in what we perceived to be their places. Forgive us for our prejudices.

O God, we need to be cleansed by your forgiveness in order to grow toward maturity. Only with clean hands and pure hearts created by your forgiving love are we able to begin seriously writing your love in our lives and conveying it to others. Help us with this responsibility. Amen.

Surprising and troubling is the correlation Jesus makes between being forgiven and forgiving others. Apparently, I cannot experience forgiveness if I do not forgive others. Why? Because I will not know forgiveness when I see it. I wonder if God ever thinks about me as I think about others. If so, God might say, "I'm tired of forgiving Howard Roberts. When I do forgive him and think he is on the way to getting his life in order, he turns right around and sins again. I've forgiven him 25,363 times. That's enough! I've been a very patient God!"

Nowhere can I find any hint that this is the attitude or approach of God. I am grateful. God's constant willingness and eagerness to forgive me are healing and transforming.

One of the most frightening daily invitations we receive is the offer to do evil. Seldom does the evil offer appear as something horrible or detestable. Rather, the invitation may come in the form of "my rights" or "why shouldn't I feel that way" or "what I do won't hurt anybody." These clues tell us that every day we need God to deliver us from doing evil. Perhaps the following prayer can express this for you:

Dear God,

Help me to sense your constant presence with me today. When difficulties arise, deliver me from giving in to evil. Deliver me from the evil of responding in kind to those who do harm to me. Help me to turn the other cheek. Keep far from me the desire to bring down, to harm, or to destroy another person. Deliver me from degrading those who out of fear for themselves do not remain as loyal as they had promised. Deliver me from the evil of selling the principles by which I have lived and the commitment I have promised for a bowl of security or a dish of approval. Deliver me from the evil of condemning another person because of the hurt I experience. Deliver me from the evil of retaliation. When I am taunted by the temptation to do something to prove my worth, deliver me from the evil of overdoing and overworking.

God, make me conscious of the daily option not to do evil, and assure me of your guidance in delivering me away from doing evil. I offer this prayer in the name of the One who teaches me to pray, Jesus the Christ. Amen.

Praying for ourselves involves communicating to God our emotional whereabouts as well as our needs. Some of our daily needs may not immediately fit in the categories of food, forgiveness, or deliverance. To pray for ourselves is to let God know exactly what is our struggle, hurt, celebration, or dream at the moment. And these will vary from moment to moment within the day.

What follow are three prayers related to different circumstances and responses I had in one day. I suspect you have had days with circumstances like mine. May the words I have used help you to pray for yourself.

> What a rich and glorious gift I was given, God! A sabbatical leave! What relief I felt when I first heard this recommendation! Just the possibility was a wonderful gift. Then for the possibility to become reality was fantastic. The planning and preparation for travel and reflection were enjoyable. The experiences afforded me during the sabbatical were more fabulous than I ever dreamed. I am astounded at the knowledge, abilities, and skills of people who lived hundreds and thousands of years ago. I am overwhelmed by the efforts people went to in constructing places of worship in order to praise and honor you. I am hurt, angered, and disturbed by the destructive and murderous things people did in your name, claiming your blessing.
>
> Two insights were continually revealed to me during this time, God: (1) how unbelievably friendly and helpful people were to me, a total stranger, and (2) how unbelievably ignorant I am. Everywhere I went I was in need of assistance with directions, and people gladly assisted. Everywhere I engaged in conversation with people, and they were open and eager to share with me and learn about me. God, you have made wonderful people all over the world, and I had the privilege of being helped by many of them.
>
> This was also a significant journey in humility. Most of the people I met were at least bilingual. I barely speak English. Too many of us in the United States have the expectation that wherever we go, people will speak our language. What delight others showed at my feeble efforts to speak their language.

God, in many ways the world got bigger and smaller at the same time for me during this sabbatical. It got bigger as I saw amazing structures that people have built through the years—cathedrals, castles, fortified cities. It got bigger as I met people from faraway places and listened to their stories. But the world also got smaller because my life connected with the lives of people who live thousands of miles away. Now I have a kinship with them, and I have faces to go with words like the Irish, the Palestinians, the Israelis.

Thank you, God, for showing me a broader perspective. Thank you for enriching my life through the lives of people I encountered. Thank you for disclosing yourself in the faces of total strangers. Thank you for demonstrating genuine hospitality through people who welcomed me into their homes and sought to befriend me.

What a wonderful gift I have been given. Please help me, dear God, to be a good steward of this wonderful gift. Amen.

Later in the day I recalled some of the circumstances that precipitated the granting of a sabbatical leave. Returning from this trip, I would be faced with the reality of those circumstances. And so I prayed for myself again in a different tone.

God,

I don't know what to say. When I think about what is happening to me, I have trouble putting it into words to you. I'm hurt. I'm angry. I'm being treated unfairly. I am the scapegoat for several people's dissatisfaction, but I can't figure out what they are dissatisfied about. Why do they want the church to meet their every need? Why do they want to hear what they already believe? Why do they want church to be a pep rally of feeling good? Why do they want church to be the happening place to go? Why did they expect me to bring all of that about? What misled them? Did I? Did they see one thing and hear another in me? Why is there not compassion on their part? Why do they seem not to care about what all of this does to me personally and professionally? Why do they act oblivious of the personal effect and impact that this has?

God, is there any way for me to get out of this gracefully? I am as clear as I have ever been that being a pastor is where my gifts lie and this is my calling. But how can I live out this calling when people do not want me to be their pastor? How can this congregation minister effectively when there are people resisting—a few actively and several passively? Some have made up their minds that the congregation cannot be effective as long as I am pastor. So much for the priesthood of all believers.

God, is there another place where I can work? I know that wherever I go, you will be there to work with me and through me. Please help me to find a place that will benefit from my abilities, a people that I can nurture and challenge, and a place that will appreciate and love me, a place that will nurture and challenge me. God, I need such a place right now. Amen.

Nearly every day someone crosses my path, and the encounter is disturbing at best and infuriating at worst. Such an encounter occurred on the same day as the events that led to the previous two prayers. This encounter fell somewhere between disturbing and infuriating. In any case, here is what I said to God about it:

God,

I was angered and saddened by the man I met today. The encounter began simply and innocently. I was obviously seeking to find my way. He perceived I was unsure of which way to go. He asked if he could help. I told him where I wanted to go. He said he would take me there. What better offer is there for giving directions than to have someone go with you to the place?

He wanted to know where I was from. "Alabama? Is George Wallace still alive? George Wallace has been here. Do you have children?" I told him three. He said he had seven. By now we've wandered a long way, and I knew enough about the area that we had wandered the long way around. We arrived at the place. I thanked him and then he wanted some money. I refused. He cursed and spit at me. He ordered me to leave his country and never return.

I was angered that what at first appeared to be hospitality was no more than hustling for change. I was saddened that a tourist was seen as someone to use for a few coins. God, how can exchanges like this be more than this? What can I do in chance encounters to make a difference for the better in the other person's life? What may I permit the other person to do to make a difference for the better in my life?

O God, forgive me if I in any way mistreated or misled this man. May he forgive me if I hurt him in any way. May he be able to provide for the needs of his family. May he love them, and may they know that they are loved. I offer this prayer in the attitude of the One who teaches us how to love. Amen.

Pray for yourself every day. Pray openly, honestly, fervently. Know that you have a Compassionate Friend who longingly waits to hear from you and who will journey beside you through the myriad experiences of the day.

QUESTIONS TO PONDER

1. What are your thoughts and feelings about being urged to pray for yourself?
2. What correlation do think there is between loving yourself and praying for yourself?
3. What are some of the barriers that block your communing with God?
4. What is your prayer pilgrimage like? Take some time now and write your prayer pilgrimage. Reflect on it. Were there any surprises? What did you learn about your view of yourself? How has your view of God changed through your journey?
5. Identify three different experiences you had today. Write a prayer expressing your feelings, needs, hopes, and dreams related to each of these experiences.
6. Write a prayer a day whether you need it or not.

CHAPTER NINE

Praying for Friends and Enemies

MATTHEW 5:43–45

WHY DOES ANYBODY pray? Primarily, people pray because they are convinced that God listens to them.[1] The converse is true. People stop praying if they are convinced that God doesn't listen to them. People need assurance of an audience with God to continue communing with God. David Elkind suggests that the opportunity to communicate with God about one's needs and struggles may be more important than evidence that one's prayers have been answered.[2]

Throughout life we make friends and enemies. I suspect that most of us set out to make friends, and few—if any—of us intentionally strive to make enemies. However, both friends and enemies we have. Because they are a part of our lives, we cannot commune with God about our lives without praying for friends and enemies.

Jesus drew strong reactions. Some people were drawn to him; others were repelled by him. Throughout his life Jesus was making friends and enemies. If there is any integrity in Jesus as portrayed in the Gospels, then he prayed for his friends and his enemies. How he interacted with people models what praying for friends and enemies involves. Jesus instructed us to love our enemies and pray for those who persecute us (Matt. 5:44).

Focusing on the communication process with God and addressing the transaction that occurs are much more important than the motivations behind the transaction.[3] I wonder if this is part of why Jesus urged his followers to love their enemies and pray for those who persecuted them. Nothing can turn enemies away from being enemies more quickly than praying for them. Nothing can keep enemies as enemies like refusing to pray for them.

Prayer is such an intimate interaction that to pray for another person is to take that person's needs, the person's very life, into your own life and to desire the very best for that person. To pray for a person releases the person from being your enemy. The person may continue to seek to do you harm or to work against you, but you are no longer at enmity with that person. To pray for a person or group of people is to care about them.

Often we have understood prayer as an expression of our embattlement with God. We want one thing, and we perceive that God wants another. When we pray for our enemies and they remain at enmity with us, we may conclude that is God's will and thus suggest that there is a conflict between God's will and ours. Theodore Newcomb's ideas on coorientation[4] are helpful with regard to the significance of prayer being communication rather than a conflict of wills in which we are embattled with God. Coorientation is the ability to orient oneself to the subject of discussion and to another's anticipated view of this subject simultaneously. Coorientation is not seeing eye-to-eye. Rather, it is the ability to view a situation from the perspective of another.

With regard to prayer, we are able to express our needs and problems to God and, at the same time, anticipate how God will respond. Our anticipation will be influenced by our view of God and our self-esteem. Our anticipation ought also to be informed by how God has responded to others, including Jesus and other biblical people, as well as the church fathers and well-known devotionalists such as John Woolman, Evelyn Underhill, and Michael Quoist.

Our anticipation also can be informed by asking ourselves whether the response expected from God portrays God more like a loving friend or an angry beast. The closer the anticipated response is to a loving friend, the more nearly correct we are in our coorientation. When communicating with God in this manner, we may urge

God to respond in a specific way, and at the same time we may doubt that God will respond in the way we have requested. The following prayer illustrates this:

> God,
>
> Those people give me fits. Nothing I do meets their approval. Always they are looking, hoping I'll make a mistake. They sit like vultures waiting to pounce on my carcass when I stumble.
>
> Why don't you change their attitudes? Why don't you give them loving attitudes of warmth and acceptance? If you can't or won't do that, why don't you urge them to go elsewhere instead of harassing me? Amen.

Have you ever prayed such a prayer? Have you ever had such thoughts? In a sense, you have prayed this kind of prayer if you have had thoughts like these. We think thoughts we cannot control, and they interfere with the best intentions. Thinking is unceasing. We struggle with how to convert our unceasing thinking into unceasing praying. Unceasing prayer means neither thinking about God every moment nor babbling constantly to God. To pray unceasingly is to realize that all of our thoughts occur in the presence of God. We need to turn all our thoughts into conversations with God, conversations that may or may not be verbal. Then the significant question is not, What do I think? Rather, To whom do I offer my thoughts?

This seems to be the understanding of people in the Hebrew Scriptures. They talked to God as if their suffering did not matter to God. When relief from their suffering was delayed, they accused God of a lack of compassion. When their enemies were suffering, they rejoiced, saying that God was punishing them for mistreating the Israelites. They tried to bargain with God, using different approaches to get the responses they wanted. They played up to God's name and reputation.

Evident in the prayers of people in the Hebrew Scriptures is the free-flow-for-all, especially regarding their enemies. There is evidence of this free flow in the prayers of Jesus and his courageous approach to God, as he spoke imperatively and freely, letting his fears and feelings be known. We resist letting our prayers flow directly from ourselves without censoring them. We think there is potential peril in the free flow of prayer that releases emotions within us of which we may be unaware. We think we have to get the theology straight in order to commune with God. As we explore ourselves through prayer, we need to realize that God is calling to consciousness the infinite possibilities within us. We are not seeking God; rather, God seeks us, and our search is a response to the Creator who has been brooding and moving over us since the day of our creation.

Jesus prayed for his friends as indicated in John 17. Often when I am praying for friends, I also am praying for myself. I see a lot of myself in my friends. I discover that many of the issues my friends face are my issues. I hesitate being that open and vulnerable with God. That is why praying for friends is not as easy as it sounds.

I have a variety of friends. I have friends who are colleagues, confidants, confronters, mentors, and models. Technically, all ministers are my colleagues. One colleague, Ralph, is a thirty-six-year-old minister. His many pastoral skills include sensitivity to individual needs and the ability to see the community as his parish. As a result of mounting frustration, increasing conflicts, and dead-end solutions, Ralph resigned as pastor of a church and was uncertain of employment. Out of my concern for him I offered this prayer:

> The pastorate lost a good man on Easter, Sovereign God.
>
> It's strange that crucifixion happened in the church and on Easter. I guess we still believe more in crucifixion than we do in resurrection. At least that is the method we choose to deal with persons whose leadership we dislike.
>
> Not everybody could do what Ralph does, God. He not only survives in a small town, but he actually ministers to people there. He is a pastor to many who are outside the church. He really sees the community as his parish. He is involved in the Kiwanis Club and Little League baseball, ministering to people in those organizations as well as to people in the church. There is a sense in which he is appreciated and respected more by the community than by the church. It's an old scenario repeated more often than I like to admit.

God, Ralph couldn't take it any longer. He had to get out of the pastorate. He felt no support from the congregation. How devastating! He quit with no place to work but with five bodies to feed, clothe, and shelter. Was he crazy or courageous? I think he was courageous. I couldn't have done it.

Ralph will always be a pastor, won't he, God? That's what he knows how to do, and he likes ministering to people. He's had it with the church, and I don't blame him. He is angry. I would be too. God, don't let his anger sour and turn to bitterness. He resents that congregation. Help Ralph, Sovereign God, to deal appropriately with his resentment so that all of his life is not jaundiced by it.

God, you have come to many people through Ralph. There are many others to whom you can come through him. May Ralph continue to desire to be your messenger to others. Amen.

Ralph has since become a pastoral counselor in a counseling center. He is being a pastor, a messenger of God to others—just not in the traditional congregational setting.

Sometimes colleagues become soul mates. A deep level of understanding and sharing can bond people for a lifetime. My wife and I have friends like that who came into our lives through serving on a church staff together.

We could not have better friends than Jerry and Susan. Thank you, God, for gracing our lives with theirs.

We were transplants to the same city. We were ministers with the same congregation. We were at similar ages and stages of development. We fast became friends. We became parents of children within six months of one another twice. Our children became inseparable friends and have maintained a bonded relationship through more than twenty years and living great distances apart. The bonding of our children only bonded us to one another even more.

We have shared personal and professional struggles. We have celebrated accomplishments together. We have fussed and cussed together when disappointments came and when events disheartened us. We have celebrated children getting driver's licenses, high school and college graduations, engagements and marriages. We have supported one another when parents died. Is there anything they would not do for us? Is there anything we would not do for them?

Jerry and Susan have journeyed beside us for a quarter of a century and truly are friends for life. We have become soul mates. Thank you, God, for creating Jerry and Susan. Thank you for enabling us to know one another, to share so much of life together, and for making us better people because we have been befriended by two of your choice creations. Amen.

Everyone needs to have some fun in life. Fun happens when joy is present, and joy often comes through fun people in your life. We have several friends who have helped make life fun for us. We've celebrated accomplishments—ours and our children's—grieved losses, worshiped and ministered together, and interacted with one another on varying levels. They have added depth and texture to my life, and I am grateful to God for them.

What fun people Don, Jerry, Sue, Nancy, Al, Etta, Jim, Sandra, and Bob are, God! Thank you for giving them the gift of partying. Each of them knows how to enliven life. Collectively, they know what it means to celebrate life. And celebrate they do. A special occasion, like a child's wedding, provides opportunity to gather from distant homes and enjoy one another and the event to the fullest.

But people who truly celebrate life are those who do that without a special occasion. Indeed, it is party time whenever two or more of these get together in one place. What a gift you have given through these people! The number of times and the number of people whose lives have been uplifted by them are innumerable.

Significant about all of these people is that if anyone is in need, they will respond immediately. Knowing this makes it much easier to go to them for assistance, help, and support.

God, thank you for showing me how to celebrate life through my involvement with these who have the gift of partying. Thank you also for encouraging me to care genuinely for others through these who have so genuinely and lovingly cared for me. Amen.

One of the most vital services a friend provides is that of being a confidant. Within the word is its root word, "confide," which means "to trust with." According to Mark (3:13–15), one reason Jesus chose the Twelve was the value of their friendship to him. Were not the Twelve that inner circle of friends with whom Jesus shared his most intimate struggles? Did Peter, James, and John become Jesus' confidants as the ministry unfolded, the pressures mounted, and the opposition increased?

I often am not conscious of the influence and contribution another is making to my life until I begin turning my thoughts about that person into conversation with God. I also discover that what is happening in a confidant's life becomes a concern of my own. Thus, a confidant's needs become like my own. Here is an example:

God,

What a friend I have in Joe. He is willing to hear my frustrations, aggravations, excitement, and joy. In his style, he has taught me to be more candid. He is a maverick according to traditional clergy role and expectations. Sometimes people so label him as a way to avoid dealing with his challenges. Rejection is hard to take, however it comes. Thank you for keeping Joe from being resentful or bitter.

Joe taught me to leave written prayers with people as a ministry. I have found this a valuable tool. Thank you for teaching me through Joe.

Today, Sovereign God, I am most concerned about Joe because he is preparing for surgery. No matter how routine surgery is, when it is happening to someone as important to me as Joe, I am concerned, a little frightened, for him. I want the surgery to be successful, and I want the time of recuperation to be rapid and profitable for Joe.

God, I have read that you were a friend to Abraham. Paul said that even when life caved in on him, he was not without a friend. I feel that way about Joe. His friendship is a parable to me about the friendship above time. Thank you, God, for the gift of Joe's friendship and for what it tells me about your friendship to all of us. Amen.

Some friends are disturbing. The most disturbing friends are those who confront us with their perceptions of us. What relief comes as I discover that confrontation and rejection are not the same! My ability to pray for my confronter deepens our friendship.

> God, anyone could draw a graph of my joys and pains by looking at a record of my telephone calls to John. He is the friend of my extremes. I call him when I'm flying high or crawling low. Why do I think of him at those times? He seems to be part of life's balancing act for me. I'm never quite as high or quite as low at the end of our conversations as I was at the beginning. John seems to be able to mirror reality for me. Usually, that is what I need. I'm glad he cares enough to risk my rejecting him in order to confront me, which is what I need, rather than to give me superficial support.
>
> God, what surprises me about John is that time lag is never a problem. Regardless of the time and events that have transpired between calls, as soon as there is telephone contact, there is emotional connection. We get on the same frequency immediately. What John offers is seldom what I want but is invariably what I need. Maybe that is why I think of him at high and low tides. Thank you, God, for the confrontive friend that John is. Amen.

In Homer's *Odyssey,* Odysseus's loyal friend and wise adviser was Mentor. When Odysseus left home for the Trojan War, he asked Mentor to look after his son, Telemachus. Telemachus had a formal arrangement with his adviser. I am discovering my mentors in retrospect. Through mutual sharing I have become aware of some of the needs of my mentors. The following prayer reveals some things about one of them, some of my concerns for him, and indicates how some things I see in him raise issues about myself:

> Apparently George has always been a private person, God. I'm concerned about him. Is he getting what's coming to him? That seems to be my question, not his. I am amazed at his coping ability in the face of financial difficulty. He has drawn a great deal of strength from his family. He says he had his day in the sun and enjoyed it. Now life is moving in another direction. Is it better to have had and lost than never to have had at all? George seems to think so. I don't know that I could have the same outlook if I were in his situation.
>
> God, I like George a lot. He knows what church is and who church is. You speak to me every time I see him. I wish he were attending worship, but I guess that's just too public for him now. It may be too public for him forever. He is a member of my private church. Thank you, God, for George. Amen.

One of the reasons I develop a friendship is the characteristics I like that I see in another person. As the friendship grows, I begin emulating one or more of the characteristics by trying them on for size to see how they fit me. We probably are eclectic in our modeling, trying on characteristics from diverse friends. My attitude is one of gratitude for friends who have been models for me.

> Dear God,
>
> I am richly blessed with friends. I really don't know what life would be like without friends. Each contributes to who I am.
>
> Joan has the uncanny ability to speak a word of encouragement at just the right time. There are many days when I am certain that were it not for her, I would not be able to survive here. Thank you for communicating encouragement to me through Joan.
>
> Steve has contributed to my growth through his confessional preaching. Thank you for giving him that gift and for enabling him to make himself vulnerable for the benefit of others.

Ruth seems to bring out the playful child in me. In her presence I enjoy turning loose my cynical, sarcastic self. Ruth seems to have no role expectations of me. She allows, wants, insists that I be myself with her. That is refreshing, relaxing, and renewing. Thank you for Ruth's no-strings-attached friendship.

God, I am grateful for Monica's availability. Our mutual sharing is healthy and helpful and has incarnated the truth of burden bearing. Her openness and honesty are so refreshing. There is no pretense with her. I need more friends like her. I need to be more like her.

I have just begun to realize how important these relationships are to my emotional well-being and to my understanding and relationship with you, God. Thank you for wrapping and sending your availability in Joan, Steve, Ruth, and Monica. May you wrap and send one of your gifts through me to others. Amen.

Probably everybody knows someone who seems to epitomize friendship for him or her. This person seems to convey friendship in every relationship and to demonstrate qualities that any friend would like to have. The following prayer expresses gratitude for one who does this for me:

No one could be more richly blessed than I, God, to have a member of the congregation like Sylvia. Would that all ministers could be blessed at least once in their ministries with a Sylvia. What a wonderful work you have done in her, God.

What is it that makes Sylvia such a unique embodiment of your presence? Perhaps it's her music. She is gifted as a musician, and her piano interpretations of classical masterpieces and hymns move the musically and nonmusically inclined into a spirit of worship of you.

Maybe Sylvia's distinctive is her compassion. Especially sensitive to the outcasts and those on the fringes, Sylvia is never afraid to place her life alongside those being excluded and risk being excluded with them.

Openness, perhaps it is Sylvia's openness that enables her to embody your presence, God. Never does she consider that she has the truth in captivity. Never does she make anyone feel that his or her opinion or view is invalid or dumb or useless. Never does she impose her will, her desire, or her ideas onto another.

No one can express thoughts more clearly, warmly, and directly in writing than Sylvia. Her writings show depth of insight, breadth of compassion, and height of understanding.

What a good work you have done in Sylvia! Obviously, she knows you and is known by you. Apparently, the security of knowing she is loved by you is enough for her. She easily incarnates your presence to any and all who will receive your grace, compassion, and love through her. Surely, her radiance is a reflection of your love radiating to her. Thank you, God, for giving me the privilege of sharing ministry with Sylvia. May every person who ministers in your name be given the gift of a Sylvia. Amen.

Praying for friends has increased the value of friendship for me, helped me discover friends I did not know I had, and nudged me to grow toward who I want to be. Awareness of friends also has caused me to examine the kind of friend I am and want to be.

The antithesis of friends is enemies. Having enemies is not easy to admit. Most of my enemies are in the church, probably because that is where I invest most of my time and energy. Learning that I had enemies in the church shattered the idealism that I could relate well with everyone. I should have known better. Even Jesus couldn't do that!

Just as friendship requires contributions from two people, it takes two to have differences that become enmity between them. I have contributed to my enemies being my enemies. Being able to pray for my enemies is a major growth step because it is an admission of having enemies and knowing who they are. It also is a step toward ending the enmity.

There is a sense in which my enemies represent my shadow side. To begin to know my enemies is to learn some things about my darker side. And I need to keep in mind that I probably represent some of their shadow sides. An enemy's animosity toward me probably is not all because of me but is partly because of what I represent and of whom I remind that person.

My enemies include skeptics, competitors, distractors, betrayers, and antagonists. I am certain you can add to this list or find words that are more descriptive for you. I hope you will because the more specific you and I can be in identifying our enemies and what they are like, the better will be our praying for them. The greater will be our growth as well.

A skeptic is a person who has become disenchanted with me because of an issue, or just basically doesn't like me, and then continually finds fault with me. A skeptic distrusts me and functions as a sniper. She takes shots at me in the presence of others but does not say anything to me. Here is a prayer I offered for one skeptic:

Dear God,

My struggle with Marian has been so difficult. I have felt for a long time that she does not listen to what I have to say. I was taken completely by surprise when she said she did not think I was a good fit as pastor for the congregation. Then I was startled when she said that she was not suggesting that I resign but was asking me to consider what I thought would be the best solution for the church. I was very angry with her when she would not at least name a complaint she had against me. Her deceptiveness was made more apparent in her actions in public meetings.

I really don't know what to do about Marian or with her. I am convinced that nothing I do is satisfactory to her. It seems so difficult for her when she realizes how differently she and I see an issue or understand a passage of Scripture. I guess she equates acceptance with agreement. I used to do that too. I think freedom is difficult for Marian, too, God. If all of life could just be orderly and structured so that there would be no surprises, she would be more at ease. But life isn't that way.

Is there any way I can help her with this struggle? What does Marian need, God? Like all of us, she needs your grace and mercy. How can I help deliver these gifts to her? Will Marian trust me enough to permit us to struggle together? I wish she would. Will it ever happen? O God, whatever the wounds, whatever the needs in Marian's life, heal them. Make her whole and give her peace. Amen.

Culture encourages competition. Then jealousy and envy set in. We move into the destructive mood. The jealous competitor says, "If I don't have what you have, I will fight you every step of the way to make you miserable." The envious competitor says, "If I can't have what you have, I'll destroy you so you can't have it either."

God,

I don't like Sam's scowl. He seems so unhappy, so angry. At times I am convinced he hates me. There are times when I am certain he would delight in destroying me. Please protect me from allowing my paranoia to rule me.

I have trouble admitting there is someone to whom I can't minister, but Sam is one. I do not struggle much when someone disagrees with me, but sugarcoated, mean-spirited disagreement is hard for me to handle. I get angry. I feel threatened. I do a lot of looking over my shoulder. There was a time when I was immobilized, but you helped me through that. I thought things would get better, and they have. I guess I wanted things to get well, and that may never happen. I feel better admitting that. It really hurts when Sam avoids speaking to me. Is there a part of me that is like him? If so, help me to change. Deliver me from doing to Sam what I feel he has done to me. Amen.

Regardless of our situations, there usually is someone attempting to distract us from our focus. On one occasion in Jesus' ministry, Peter was the distractor. Jesus said to him, "Get behind me, Satan! You are a stumbling block to me; for you are setting your mind not on divine things but on human things" (Matt. 16:23). The distractor may be one who is emotionally needy calling selfishly for time and attention for herself or getting me to pursue his set of priorities.

The primary tool of a distractor is manipulation, and the most difficult thing to do in dealing with a distractor is to be angry but not sin. Being able to name these things in communion with God helps me deal with a distractor.

O God,

I know that Mary is dissatisfied with me. Some days I feel that the only solution is to call her up and ask what she thinks I should do today. Whatever I do without her consent I know will be wrong. Why is she like this? Why does everything always have to go Mary's way or be judged worthless, if not verbally, then by her actions and facial expressions? I get so angry with her, I just want to lash out at her. Sometimes I'm afraid I'll lose control of myself and verbally unload on her in public. My private conversations with Mary have gotten me nowhere.

Treating her with kindness has helped me. Of course, sometimes my kindness has been a sarcastic, I'll-fix-you attitude. Forgive me for that. Help me to communicate genuine concern for Mary. Make her aware of some of the pain she causes me and others with her diversions and detractions. Amen.

The most painful hurt a person ever experiences may be betrayal. A betrayal experience tends to declare all of one's life null and void. When someone who has trusted has broken that trust, a friend can become an enemy. The following prayer expresses the gamut of feelings that mushroom from an encounter with a betrayer:

God, I'm tempted to cash in my chips today. I just want to quit everything and go off somewhere alone. I feel like I'm running hard to nowhere. I want out from under it all. I started too young. I got lots of praise for being so far along for my age. Now age has caught up with me. I'm taken for granted.

God, it's lonely at the top of whatever heap I'm on. What's the use? Why spend my life doing this? Surely, there is more to life than listening to people complain about budgets and offerings and orders of worship. Where is the sacred part of my life—the part that nobody attacks or hurts, the part that is vulnerable to no one and no thing? I am naked and exposed. There is no protection. I'm tired of being considered so strong, as if I had no feelings.

I have been betrayed, not by accident, not by uncontrollable circumstances, but by willful intent. God, this hurts in a strange way. I guess this is what I want to talk to you about. It's all expressed to me in a "you'll understand and accept this" kind of way. I ought to want to lash out, get even, hurt back, destroy, make Jack pay, but I feel none of these. Maybe I'm too numb to feel anything. I don't like the notion, "He'll get over this and everything will be okay." I feel bitter, and I sense I'm slipping into despair, even apathy. How can this be happening to me? I've been kidding myself. The fool at the party is me. I've been used. I've been lied to. I feel laughed at, spit on, stepped on, kicked.

I guess I'm moralizing now, God, but I think I know how you feel when I betray you. Yet following those times I have never felt unwanted or unloved by you. That is a warm, supportive surprise. On the one hand, I want to be loving and accepting toward Jack, who betrayed me. On the other hand, I don't want to run the risk of being betrayed again. What guarantees do I have? What guarantees do you have about my trustworthiness? God, help me forgive Jack. Please forgive me for betraying you. Amen.

An antagonist is one whose attitude or state of mind is in active opposition to a person or issue. The antagonistic enemy is obvious, perhaps even blatant in opposition. Facial expressions and voice inflections convey antagonism.

Often the antagonist is a trap setter. She asks questions to which she already knows the answers, at least the answers she wants. She hopes to be able to say, in her mind at least, in hearing my answer, "Now I gotcha."

On more than one occasion, the Pharisees attempted to trap Jesus with their questions. They expected either/or answers. Jesus surprised them every time with at least a third alternative. It is significant that Jesus was more like the Pharisees than any of the religious leaders of his day. Yet they were his antagonists.

I feel helpless in the presence of an antagonist. Admitting my helplessness aids me in realizing that I cannot do everything. Then I am freed to discover there are some things I can do.

O God,

I don't know what to do about it—it all seems so useless. Before I even get the first sentence of the sermon out of my mouth, Roseanne is squirming and fidgeting. That grin on her face is so forced. It seems to be covering animosity and hostility. I used to think Roseanne had become like this only in recent years, but some of her conversations lately indicate that she has always disliked me. It is painful and difficult for me to discover and admit that someone really despises me.

Being able to say all of this to you, God, seems to help. I don't feel antagonistic toward her. I can't identify any secret desire to get back at her. Sometimes I go out of my way to speak to Roseanne and to be friendly just because I think she is avoiding me. I am amazed at how calm I can be with her. Thank you, God, for helping me to do that. Please help Roseanne get the antagonistic poison out of her system. She is destroying herself, and I don't want her to do that. Is there any way we can reach Roseanne? Can she be saved? Amen.

Praying like Jesus involves praying for ourselves but quickly expands to praying for friends and enemies. The key is the discovery that praying like Jesus involves the psychology of communication rather than the psychology of will. To live a life of prayer means to be open-eyed to myself and see my neediness, brokenness, and godlessness and to see others and the world as they are. A life formed by prayer is one formed by the sober truth. Pretense is no longer necessary because it is no longer worth the trouble.

In praying for friends and enemies, I have discovered that nothing human is alien to me. My friends and my enemies are my brothers and sisters. If I address my godlessness to God, I cannot be thankful that I am not like others. I can only plead, "God, be merciful to me, a sinner." The result is solidarity formed with my friends and enemies. In praying for them, I identify with their joys, pain, brokenness, and godlessness. Growth and healing come through friendly/enemy praying.

QUESTIONS TO PONDER

1. Is it difficult for you to pray for friends? Why or why not?
2. Identify two friends. Write a prayer for each of them. Consider sharing your prayer with them.
3. What keeps people from praying for enemies?
4. What happens to you when you pray for your enemies?
5. Who is your worst enemy?
6. Write a prayer for one of your enemies. What happened to you as you wrote this prayer?
7. Go to a quiet, private place and read orally the prayer you wrote for your worst enemy. What happened to you as you were reading or after you completed reading this prayer?
8. When you pray for friends and enemies, how are you praying for yourself?

CHAPTER TEN

Grief Praying

PSALM 6:6–7

No one lives long before becoming acquainted with grief. There are numerous options available to us, and with every choice we make there is a corresponding loss. The death of a significant person in our lives is the most traumatic cause of grief. There also are losses caused by accident or the actions of others over which we have no control. Grief is a universal experience. It may be in the midst of these experiences that we discover the truth of Paul's statement that we have moanings and groanings too deep for words. Grief praying is a process of praying our way through our losses. Grief praying cannot change anything that has happened to us, but it may change how we feel about and how we deal with what has happened to us.

Jesus certainly was acquainted with grief. He cried at the death of Lazarus. On at least one occasion he cried when he saw Jerusalem and prayed, "If you, even you, had only recognized on this day the things that make for peace! But now they are hidden from your eyes" (Luke 19:42). No doubt there were other times when grief praying was part of Jesus' day.

Grief begins the moment a person becomes aware of a loss and continues until that person has assimilated the meaning of the loss into life and readjusted to a normal pattern of living. The causes of grief are multiple. The adjustment to the loss is a process of changes and movements. A wealth of material has been published in recent years concerning grief. Differing lists of the stages of grief have been compiled ranging from Cassem's two stages[1] to Westberg's ten stages.[2] I have identified six stages in the grief process: shock, numbness, fantasy, depression, stabbing pain, and readjustment. Awareness of these stages helps our grief praying. The following prayer expresses some of the emotions any loss may precipitate:

> God,
>
> I feel like I have lived a lifetime in the last seven days. Crisis events are like that. They cause a gamut of feelings, better described as an emotional roller coaster. One moment I was in the valley of despair. The next moment I was climbing the peak of exhilaration, only suddenly to feel like I was being flung over the brink into emptiness. Seemingly, the least significant event became paramount. I wanted to examine every detail. A word like "mainly" spoken in conversation required interpretation.
>
> Much of my life has been up for review. It may have been the most intense week of my life. I have a very different view of life this Monday than last. Last Monday I felt nothing. Today I am on a mountain, looking out at the terrain and seeing a road marked "Hope," which I shall travel. Last week only intellectually was I confident of your presence. In reflection, I realize I felt an undergirding. That was you, wasn't it, God? Today, I sense you out ahead, pulling me toward you. I am eager to be drawn by you. I know the journey will have both sorrow and joy. I am willing to risk the sorrow to experience the joy. In some way the two are related. A college student said it best, "If there is no pain in the goodbye, there can be no joy in the hello."
>
> I guess we constantly are saying goodbye to one part of life and hello to another. Graduations, marriages, births, and deaths are mixtures of goodbyes and hellos. Marriage and family conflict call for saying goodbye to situations as they used to be or we dreamed they would be and hello to the way things are. There is pain. There is joy. Thank you for being God of my pain and God of my joy in the lifetime I have lived this week. Amen.

You probably can identify with some portion of this prayer. That is evidence that all of us are the grievers, and there is grief at every stage of life. Praying like Jesus means communing with God about the pain that our losses cause. Believe it or not, there is grief at weddings. The tears are part of the evidence. Here is a prayer for persons grieving at a wedding:

> We are grateful, God, that John and Susan invited us to celebrate with them the most important day in their lives. Their nervousness and ours indicate something of the significance and seriousness of marriage.
>
> Thank you, God, for the gift of life in the beautiful packages of John and Susan. Thank you that their parents sought to nurture and guide John and Susan out of dependence upon them and into dependence upon you.
>
> Their parents are delighted for John and Susan, and yet there is some pain. It is hard for them to imagine that these they held in their arms are now ready to hold each other. It seems only yesterday that John and Susan were running to mom and dad to show them the gap where a tooth was or crying out for the comfort of a parent's lap because of a scraped knee. It doesn't seem that long ago that John didn't notice girls and Susan didn't notice boys. Now their eyes sparkle when they look at each other. Support their parents as they say goodbye to the son or daughter they once knew and hello to the man or woman each is becoming.
>
> God, John's and Susan's brothers and sisters are glad and sad today. They are glad for John and Susan because they want to give themselves in marriage to each other. Their brothers and sisters are sad for themselves. Right now they feel like they are losing a part of themselves, and that is an empty feeling.
>
> We have heard it said that at marriage a man and a woman are to leave their families and give themselves to each other. John and Susan want to do that, God, but they cannot without some pain and struggle. They are saying goodbye to a life they have known and hello to a life together that is unknown. They are excited and frightened. Calm their fears, God, with your presence and guidance. As they commit themselves to each other, may they promise not only

to allow but also to help each other to grow. May they be encouragers to each other. May their love for you and for each other deepen each day and burn away the impurities in their lives. May their youthful fascination grow toward mature charm. As time and trials leave traces upon their faces, may they keep holding hands in the dark, keep reaching for each other, and keep tuning their love.

Now, O God, may your love that will not let us go enrich John and Susan and give them hope and help today and every day for as long as they live. Amen.

When a child is born, there are hello and goodbye—hello to new life and goodbye to what life was like without the new responsibility. Prayer at such a time might be like this:

Eternal Lover of children, thank you that Jim and Joan could be partners with you in the life-giving process. They are delighted that Susie is a healthy, full-term infant. They are eager to be the kind of parents Susie needs.

God, Jim and Joan have some ambivalent feelings about this new, unknown stage of life. Although they decided together to be parents and have spent the last nine months preparing for Susie's arrival, they have some feelings that trouble them. Already they miss those quiet evenings by the fire when it was just the two of them. They are fearful that Susie will come between them. Help them, dear God, to love Susie but not to dote on her. Help Jim and Joan to continue to find time for each other. That won't be as easy now, but don't let them give up. May they see that the best way for Susie to feel secure and loved is for them to continue nurturing their love for each other.

Sometimes they may wish they didn't have Susie. Let them know you understand. When they recall the "good old days," help them to season those memories with a large dose of reality and to go light on the nostalgia.

God, now Jim and Joan will be parents for as long as they live, and they will be spouses that long too. May they be honest with their feelings of loss as they journey through the change so they may in the proper way and at the proper time say goodbye to the newlywed phase of their lives and hello to the parenting phase. I offer this prayer in the manner in which I think Jesus would pray. Amen.

Parents have their children only for a season, and then the children leave their homes of origin and form homes of their own. For many the jolt is felt when the last child leaves home. They have invested themselves in those who have left. A part of themselves is gone. The "nest" is empty, and it takes some grieving to adjust. The following prayer expresses some of my concerns for one couple who were "empty nesters":

God,

Bob and Carol are struggling. They don't seem to have any motivation. Sometimes they don't seem to know what to do with themselves. There's nothing on television. They barely scan the newspaper. When they go out to eat, they just dawdle over their food, like the kids used to do. That's where the pain is, isn't it, God?

The kids are grown and gone. That's what Bob and Carol wanted to happen, but it hurts. I saw it in their eyes when I mentioned Susan's name. Then they put it into words. For years their house was too small; now it's too big. How many meals did they eat complaining about the noise and wishing for some peace and quiet? They have the quiet now, but they don't sense any peace. Their house hasn't been this quiet for twenty-five years.

God, this is a difficult time of transition for Bob and Carol. They get on each other's nerves. Now that they have uninterrupted time for each other, they seem only to want to talk about the kids being gone, and that hurts so much that they don't talk about it. God, help them to talk about their pain and to discover through their painful dialogue that they have more to talk about than their children. Guide them to talk about each other, and help them to renew the romance of their marriage. Bob and Carol both feel the pain of their loss. May their pain be an entrance to a relationship of deeper commitment to each other rather than an exit leading to a broken relationship. Amen.

I have never met a person who was divorcing who was not hurting, regardless of the circumstances. One of the most significant things I can do for divorcing people is to pray for them. To pray for them is to embrace them, take their pain and hurt as my own and communicate with God about the agony that is experienced.

O Eternal Healer of wounds, after fourteen years of marriage, Pat and Sue are calling it quits. They're cashing in their marriage chips today. When and where did they go wrong? Sue says it began years ago when she started to feel intimidated by Pat. Since he hit her, she has been frightened to disagree with him. Pat says the problems began when Sue went to work two years ago. All those women at work convinced Sue how great single life is, according to Pat.

This marriage has been in trouble a long time, and so much damage has been done that neither Pat nor Sue is willing to risk the hurt to invest in rebuilding the relationship. God, comfort them in their hurt and their lost dreams. Each of them hurts and at times wants to hurt the other in return. I see this most clearly in their arguments about custody of the children.

The children already feel in the middle. They are convinced that somehow they are responsible for this divorce. Help the children to know that isn't true. Protect Pat and Sue from damaging each other and their children any more than already has occurred.

Sometimes, God, I think they are deciding who wins and who loses by who gets the children. Help them see that there are no winners in divorce. Help Pat and Sue keep from counting the ways they have been hurt or searching for ways to hurt in return. Every month when he sends the child-support payment and she receives it, they will remember what used to be and never can be again. When the children make plans to visit him, Pat and Sue will remember. When decisions concerning the children have to be made, they will remember.

God, help Sue and Pat to admit their marriage has ended. Protect them from holding on to false hopes of reconciliation. Protect their self-esteem from erosion by guilt and self-pity. Enable them to admit their wrongs to you. Cleanse them and make them whole. Guide them in redirecting and rebuilding their lives. Help them to be whole persons, wholly committed to you. Amen.

Somewhere in the vicinity of the thirty-fifth birthday, a person realizes life is half over. Many struggle with life at the midpoint. The following prayer expresses some of my concerns for one of the midlifers I have known:

O Stable One, help Mike to know you are with him on the rocky road he is traveling. It has been a six-month roller coaster ride for Mike. Change is never easy, but midlife career change seems to create stress as nothing else does. For twenty-seven years Mike worked for the same employer. Why did he get out? There are many factors, but a strong one was the clear message that he didn't fit in with the current program. That hurts. I get angry for him and with him.

I'm glad he has retirement income, but that doesn't compensate for over-the-shoulder looking, second-guessing, and what-am-I-going-to-do-with-the-rest-of-my-life feelings. His life has been structured for years, and now it is almost totally unstructured. Some mornings he feels very brave, but by noon he wishes he weren't so brave. Other mornings he just feels numb, and by noon he is down on every decision he has ever made.

He wants a job, but not just any job. He left just any job, which is what it had become, because he was not using his skills. His next job needs to be fulfilling and to have purpose. This raises the question of worth. Mike raises it. No one else does. Friends reveal their insensitivity when they ask, "Are you working? Did you get a job yet?"

JoAnn doesn't know what to do. She isn't used to Mike being home for dinner on time. It's nice having him around, and sometimes it's not so nice. JoAnn is adjusting too.

Mike and JoAnn seem to have an abundance of energy. They are looking for worthwhile investments. Help them, God, to find constructive channels for their energy and gifts so they will be good stewards of their time, energy, and gifts. May they find worth together in being rather than in doing so that your grace may permeate their lives. Amen.

We are people on the move. We move geographically, socially, vocationally, spiritually. All moves do not result in geographical uprooting, but they are painful changes nevertheless. One example is a church staff member who resigned his position because of health problems and remained an active participant in the congregation. Here is a prayer I offered for him and for us:

Dear God,

It was a very good day when Leonard Lane became assistant to the pastor. "Supportive" is a word that describes Leonard. He is an encourager, a modern-day Barnabas (son of encouragement).

During these thirteen years Leonard has been a present help in time of trouble. God, I am grateful for the help and hope you have given to others through Leonard. Thank you for the support and encouragement you have offered me through him.

April 30 is a very sad day. This is the day when Leonard ends his role as assistant to the pastor. This is a sad day for Leonard because it is not what he wants to do; rather, it is what he has to do for his health's sake. It really is Leonard's integrity that precipitated this decision. He could have been a hanger-on, but he could not live with himself if he were not able to give his all to the task. Leonard has been able to give of himself to others through this position. I know he will continue to give of himself, but the change causes its own sadness.

We feel the loss, too—our loss. We are comforted knowing Leonard will remain a participant in this congregation. It is easier for us to say goodbye to the position than to say goodbye to the person.

Now, O God, as Leonard leaves one phase of service and seeks to take up another, may the road rise to meet him, may the wind be always at his back, and may you continue to hold him in the palm of your hand. Amen.

The aging process has its effect on us. The wear and tear of the years begin to be felt in various parts of the body. Sometimes this is evident in repeated health problems, and grief sets in as a person is confronted repeatedly with a health issue. Ruth is one of those people. Here is a prayer I offered for her:

God,

You know that it has become increasingly difficult for Ruth to maintain a positive and encouraging outlook on life. The continued flare-ups of chest pain indicate a problem. She has been through this more times than she wants to remember and more times than most of us have counted. She has been through the trauma of open-heart surgery, which was successful.

That trauma is revisited each time she has serious chest pain. Each time she experiences this pain, her physician recommends a heart catheterization. Numerous times she has undergone this procedure. Each time she has come away with no blockage or only minor blockage.

But the anxiety is there. Ruth feels like her life is on hold. Just as she begins to get into a normal routine, her body feels okay, she is not preoccupied with what may be wrong with her body or what may be happening to her, the pain returns, the catheterization is recommended, and the cycle is repeated.

I don't know how many more times Ruth can go through this, God. She has fought off the doldrums and the discouragement for a long time, but that battle is becoming more difficult. Thank you, God, for constantly being with Ruth, for giving her courage, and for assuring her with your hope. Help her to cope physically and mentally with all the issues that the first sense of chest pain raises for Ruth. Help her to know of your abiding care for her. May her body respond to treatment and exercise in a way that frees her from pain and undergirds her with hope, hope in you, O God. Amen.

The aging process may interrupt dreams and halt plans. The following prayer expresses my concern for a couple whose retirement plans were altered radically because of disease:

God,

Emajean and Bob need your help and hope. They had exciting plans for retirement. Trips to take, stamps and coins to organize, flowers and vegetables to raise. Now they can't do any of these things.

Bob has struggled with Parkinson's disease for ten years. Then the hyperglycemia developed. Now Bob's mind does not function as it once did. He was such a bright person, a small, caring, quiet, organized man who got the job done. Now he can follow only one brief instruction at a time, if that.

At times Emajean cannot bear to admit what she is seeing and feeling. Now she has retired to take care of Bob. This wasn't what she had planned for retirement. Her patience runs out by noon every day. Forty years ago when she said, "For better or for worse, in sickness and in health," she did not know that "worse" and "sickness" meant this.

Will Bob's illness consume Emajean as it has consumed him? O God, Emajean needs your help. Sustain and strengthen her today. Bob has degenerated rapidly in the last four years. At times he is only a trembling shell. What hope does Emajean have? She can reminisce about how things used to be. That results in anger. She can recall the support Bob was to her during the years she battled cancer. That obligates her. She can anticipate Bob's death. That saddens her. She can plan what she will do after Bob dies. That makes her feel guilty. She can bring all these things to you, and she does.

Emajean has trouble on every hand, but she knows she is not without friends. She is working at living one day at a time, and it is work. It is difficult for her not to worry about tomorrow, but she is learning that she cannot face tomorrow without the resources of today. She needs your help to live all of today before she tries to live tomorrow.

There is hope for Emajean, and it rests in you. Thank you, God. Amen.

If we live very long, we will have opportunity to visit with someone who is dying. Being with dying people has sensitized me to their needs. Usually, what they want are strength and courage for living the days they have. They want to be as comfortable as possible, and they do not want to be a burden to anyone. When life can no longer be lived with dignity and meaning, they want to die. Being able to pray for the dying with these things in mind is helpful for the dying, for their family and friends, and for me.

Recently, I visited a man in the hospital whom I had known for five years. He had been battling cancer for seven years and had had several remissions. The day of this visit, I was not certain that he was conscious, but when I spoke, he replied. Before leaving, I asked him if he wanted me to have a prayer, and he said "Yes." As I held his hand, this is the prayer I offered for him. I don't know who was strengthened the most through our communion with God—the man, his wife and daughters who were in the room, or me.

Dear God,

You have been a constant source of strength to Everett through this journey, and we are very grateful for that. There is a sense in which this is the most difficult day of Everett's life, a day of saying goodbye to this family. There are three things that he needs today, God. He needs help, hope, and strength. All of these things you can give him. Give them to him today. Amen.

As I said "Amen," Everett firmly gripped my hand as if to shake hands and said "Amen," which means "So be it." Everett died later that evening.

My profession puts me in contact with people who are dying and with their families and friends who are bereaved. As a pastor, I develop relationships with members of the congregation. I am affected by what happens to them. Not long ago, I received the news that a friend who lives in another city had died. I served as her pastor many years earlier. She had maintained contact with me through the years. When I learned of her death, here is how I responded:

> God,
>
> I lost a wonderful friend when Lucille James died. I really expected her to recover from the stroke. The initial signs were that she was making great positive progress. I even sent her a card to her house, anticipating she would be home by the time the card arrived. I am sad that her life ended. I wasn't ready for this. No one ever is.
>
> I will miss her telephone calls. They always came as a pleasant surprise. There was no pattern or schedule in the timing of her calls. There was a pattern, however, to the nature of her calls. God, you know that her calls were always motivated by her care and compassion for my family and me and wondering how we were. Thank you, God, for Lucille's care and compassion.
>
> My life was uplifted by conversations with her. Being cared for does that. God, there was always a sense of your presence in conversations with Lucille. She incarnated your care and compassion. Thank you for giving me a friend like Lucille. Thank you for making yourself known to me through her. Thank you for the many others you came to through Lucille. Help me to be for others what Lucille was for me. Amen.

I have identified some of the grief-causing experiences common through the ages and stages of life. No doubt you can think of others. Grief is the emotional response people make to loss, and no one is exempt. The grief process is an occasion for us to commune with God. It is a time for us to do grief praying. Perhaps when we pray for the grievers, more than at any other time, we are praying for ourselves.

QUESTIONS TO PONDER

1. What grief experiences do you think Jesus had in addition to the two I mentioned at the outset of this chapter?
2. What was your last grief experience?

3. What were the form, shape, and sounds of your grief praying?
4. Name someone you know who is in the midst of grief. Write a prayer for that person. Consider giving the written prayer to that person. You may be surprised at what a source of strength your prayer will be.

CHAPTER ELEVEN

Praying Is Worship

PSALM 107:1–3

Authentic prayer may be unadulterated worship. When we are communing with God, pouring out our lives to God, we are giving ourselves totally to God. At these times we are giving ultimate worth, allegiance, and commitment to God. Praying, then, is worship, and the prayers of worship can help us worship God. Praying like Jesus helps us to worship God privately and publicly.

Evidence abounds in the Gospels that Jesus regularly participated in synagogue and temple throughout his life. Prayer was an integral part of worship in synagogue and temple. No doubt Jesus participated in public prayers in public worship. The book of Psalms was the hymnbook and the prayer book all rolled into one. In the Psalms is evidence that prayer is worship and genuine worship is authentic prayer.

George Buttrick, an outstanding Presbyterian pulpiteer, said that for every minute he spent in the pulpit, he spent an hour in preparation. A significant part of his preparation involved the prayers to be offered in public worship. He said, "If you must choose between getting the sermon right and getting the prayers right, get the prayers right!"[1]

Worship is an event, an encounter between the living God and those who desire to be the people of God. Worship is not "going to church." It is taking our places in the congregation and contributing ourselves in appreciation to God and communion with God. Worship is the only thing we can do to God, and thus, the entire public worship event is a prayer to God. Much of the praying that occurs in public worship is public prayer because the prayers are overheard by others. James Martineau suggested our need for public prayers when he said that the tender voices of the spirit are easily lost; therefore, we need to overhear one another.

Public prayer helps people center their thoughts because there is a leveling of life through prayer. For many worshipers, the public prayers of worship aid in calming their restlessness. Augustine's truth surfaces: "We are restless until we rest in Thee." Public prayer assists us in attaching our minds and hearts to the One with whom we are eager to relate.

Prayer offered in public, regardless of the form, thaws our personal loyalties and indifference and puts us in community. Thus, public prayer is both observation and revelation. Prayer serves as both a microscope and a telescope. Public prayer as a microscope helps us see and admit that we are not perfect. As a telescope, public prayer causes us to see many needs and to discover that our needs and struggles are universal. Public prayer as revelation is a time when we express to God something of who we are. We do that individually as we identify with what is expressed through the public prayers. We do that as a community of faith because the prayers are expressions for all of us gathered to worship God. The more we reveal of ourselves, the more receptive we are to God's disclosure to us.

More than any other aspect of public worship, public prayer helps us understand genuine worship. Authentic prayer is directed to God, and there is the cue for us. Søren Kierkegaard appropriately described worship as a drama where members of the congregation are the actors, the worship leaders are the prompters, and God is the audience.

Public prayer is rehearsal. The word "rehearsal" is of French derivation and means "to harrow again," originally in the sense of breaking up and leveling plowed ground. Public prayer is rehearsal as it churns, disturbs, and makes us uncomfortable so that in private prayer we will commune with God about personal issues.

This understanding of public prayer calls for serious preparation of public prayers. This involves thinking through what one will address to God in prayer and may include writing prayers for public worship. Congregations that use a prayer book have written prayers to be used in worship. The psalms have been used as prayers for centuries. The content of many of the psalms suggests they were first private prayers that came to express publicly the needs, joys, fears, and hopes of a community of faith seeking to serve and worship God faithfully.

In developing prayers for public worship, every effort needs to be made to compose and shape ones that are true to the ways of God and faithful to the needs of people. Often as preparation for prayer is made, the person discovers that the prayer prepares her or him.

I often have conversations with people who are struggling with prayer. They feel a need to pray. They want to experience a closeness to God, and they sense that in some way this intimacy with God is related to prayer. Some want nothing more than a magic formula, which at best becomes vain repetition. One of the best opportunities to assist people in their intimate relationship with God is through the prayers of public worship. Here is where modeling of prayer occurs for the individual; thus, public prayer is rehearsal for private prayer. Perhaps that was why Buttrick insisted that we get the prayers right.

As I prepare prayers for public worship, I attempt to envision the needs of the congregation. In my mind, I walk the aisles of the sanctuary, visualizing members of the congregation, recalling what their faces say to me, and remembering their joys and sorrows, their accomplishments and struggles. Then I consider how these concerns may be common to all of us and how they can be expressed to God through prayer while respecting the anonymity of congregants.

Part of my preparation for prayer includes consideration of community, national, and world events that impact congregants' lives. Formulating concerns about these events is part of praying for public worship, and the praying is worship.

A variety of types and styles of prayers may be used in public worship. Prayer in public worship serves a priestly function because it is the vehicle for presenting the people's situations to God. The variety of prayers for public worship includes calls to worship, invocations, offertory prayers, pastoral prayers, and benedictions. What follow are comments about and illustrations of these types of prayers.

The call to worship summons people to unite in corporate worship. The call to worship is a prayer in the sense that congregants are invited to dedicate themselves to God through worship. Passages of Scripture, especially some of the psalms, may be adapted as calls to worship.

Leader:	*Praise God, my soul,*
Congregation:	*And do not forget how kind God is.*
Leader:	*God forgives all my sins,*
Congregation:	*And heals all my diseases.*
Leader:	*God keeps me from the grave,*
Congregation:	*And blesses me with love and mercy.*
Leader:	*God does not punish us as we deserve,*
Congregation:	*Or repay us for our sins and wrongs.*
Leader:	*As far as the east is from the west,*
Congregation:	*So far does God remove our sins from us.*
Leader:	*As kind as parents are to their children,*
Congregation:	*So kind is God to those who honor God.*
Leader:	*God knows what we are made of;*
Congregation:	*God remembers that we are dust.*
Leader:	*For those who honor God, God's love lasts forever,*
Congregation:	*And God's goodness endures for all generations.*
Leader:	*God's throne is placed in heaven;*
Congregation:	*God rules over all. Praise God. Praise God, O my soul!* (adapted from Psalm 103)

There are occasions when one person voices the call to worship for all worshipers. Here is an example:

> We come together to worship God as eagerly as Jesus of Nazareth strode toward the Jordan River. The faith of Jesus plunged him into the water. May our faith immerse us in worship and enable us to

wade into the deep waters of life with confidence and hope. May our journey through this worship service model for us our journey of living this week. We come to worship God eagerly and faithfully. Amen.

The invocation is a prayer directing the worshipers' attention to God and communicating to God the intentions of the congregants in worship. Through the mood and commitment of prayer, the invocation expresses worshipers' intention to be present to God, who is present to them.

Burst upon our lives, O God, like the sunlight bursting on a new day.
Warm our bodies with the rays of your love.
Brighten our vision with the light of your justice.
Penetrate our darkness with the beams of your mercy,
Embrace our disharmony with the spectrum of your peace.
Dilate our understanding with the rainbow of your hope.
Burst upon our lives, O God, like the sunlight bursting on a new day. Amen.

The variety of needs of the members of the congregation may be collected in the invocation as an expression of what they need and what their intentions are as they gather for worship. The following invocation seeks to do that:

Come to us now, O God, because our lives are sick and need your healing.

Come to us with your vision because our eyes are blind from greed.

Come to us with your hearing because our ears are deaf from self-interest.

Come to us with your speaking because our mouths are mute from dishonesty.

Come to us with your feeling because our sensitivities are stifled from selfishness.

Come to us now, O God, because our lives are sick and need your healing. Amen.

Our money is a symbol of our earnings and represents the fruit of our labor. We would not have labor were it not for the grace of God. Therefore, we could not have fruit for labor without labor. An offering is the tangible deposit from our labors that we can give regularly to the service of God through the church. The offering is a way of giving ourselves to God, and it symbolizes our personal commitment to God.

An offertory sentence or prayer is given before or after the offering is received to declare that what we do in giving is not simply a financial transaction, but a service to God. The offertory sentence or prayer focuses attention on the Giver of all gifts and is a collective expression of gratitude.

God,

We claim to be your servants in devotion and worship. May the attitude with which we give our offerings demonstrate the depth of our devotion and the height of our worship. May we always give you the first and the best of what we have. May what we give and how we give reflect our devoting all that we are and have to you. Amen.

The pastoral prayer never is to be a presentation of the pastor's soul; rather, the pastoral prayer attempts to gather the needs of the congregation and to relate these needs to the terms of the truth of the Christian gospel and to current conditions. Perhaps this prayer would be identified better as the congregational prayer. This is the one prayer in the context of public worship that may be rounded out in all dimensions of prayer—adoration, thanksgiving, confession, petition, intercession, and dedication. This prayer, as all other prayers, must never be done for its beauty; its aim is to draw out from the congregation thoughtful worship and dedication given only to God. The world of nature, current events, and other situations may contribute to our awareness of God and be reflected in the pastoral prayer. Two examples are included here:

> Almighty and merciful God, your bountiful care for us continually evokes praise and thanksgiving from our lives. Your love for us pricks our consciences and creates awareness of our dependence on you. Thank you for loving us and caring for us even when we have been unloving and uncaring.
>
> God, we confess to you that we have not loved our neighbors as ourselves because we have not loved ourselves. We have done many things that show hatred for ourselves. We overwork our minds and bodies and damage ourselves with undue pressure. We excessively take things into our bodies that destroy the health and vitality of our lives. Then when a product is taken off the market, we scream loudly because of the inconvenience it is causing us. Much of what we do and what we consume proclaims that we do not love ourselves.
>
> We do not love our neighbors either. We don't even know them. We don't take the time to find out who people are, much less what are their needs that we may help them meet. God, how much good have we ever done for someone who disliked us or hated us? We know the answer. It is painful to admit that we have wronged so many. We cry for mercy and forgiveness for ourselves, but when others ask the same of us, we become cold, indifferent, and merciless. O God, great is our sin, but even greater are your grace and forgiveness. Please forgive us our trespasses, and help us to forgive those who trespass against us.
>
> God, multiple are the needs of others. The effects of war remain ever with us. The physical injuries, the emotional scars, the spiritual wrenching tear at the fabric of our lives. We mourn the hurt and lifelong losses that war brings.
>
> God, people everywhere are clamoring to be treated as persons. Family members often treat one another as less than human. People of different races treat one another differently because of skin pigmentation. People of different nations treat one another differently because of their language differences. O God, the needs of people

often are overwhelming. Help us to be part of the solution rather than part of the problem.

God, help us to renew our promises to you and to keep the promises we make. We give ourselves to you as instruments through whom you can speak and minister. In the name of Christ, we pray. Amen.

O Giver of refreshment, as the gentle rain soaks the earth, may we be soaked in the gentle messages of love you constantly are beaming to us. As new life bursts forth from well-prepared and well-watered soil, may we be well nourished so that new life may burst forth in us and through us.

We know that sin scorches our lives and makes them barren. We know that your forgiveness is the only oasis for our dry and parched lives. Hear our confessions of sins, O God. We have done wrong, but we have blamed it on others. Forgive us. We have benefited from the hurt done to another and enjoyed it. Forgive us. We have passed on information that was entrusted to us. Forgive us. We have refused to look into the eyes of hungry people. Forgive us. We have refused to touch people who are sick. God, forgive us. We have avoided bereaved and dying people. Forgive us. Create clean hearts in us, O God. Restore us, remake us, and remold us as your people. As you forgive us, as you remake us, may our lives be nourished by your grace and presence.

May our lives be prepared to be your servants. May new life burst forth in us and through us, O God, our Creator and Redeemer and Sustainer. Amen.

The term "benediction" means "well speaking" and is a prayer aimed at confirming the decisions, inspiration, and instruction that have occurred in worship with the hope we will carry them from the sanctuary and implement them in the experiences and tasks of the week.

Be assured as you leave this worship place that the God you worshiped here will be with you every day. Now may the God who invited us here, who has sustained us in our worship, who has forgiven us our sins, and who has renewed the promise never to leave us or forget about us direct our living in the home place and the workplace today and every day. Amen.

Throughout the year there are special days and seasons of worship as well as special events in the lives of congregants that shape public worship. Prayers reflect the significance of these special events in the lives of worshipers such as parent-child dedication, baptism, communion, and rite of passage for sixteen-year-olds.

One of the most challenging tasks for which people are the least prepared is parenting. It is a time of change and opportunity for support of new parents and extended family members. Support from a congregation may be offered through a parent-child dedication portion of a worship service. Here is a prayer for such an occasion:

Dear Mother and Father of us all,

We thank you for the hands and hearts of the mothers and fathers who birthed and sustained Tom and Joan out of helplessness into dependency on you. May the influence of grandparents contribute to Annette's growth and maturity. May Grandmother's house be a place of refuge for her when she thinks Mom and Dad do not understand. Thank you, God, for Annette's grandparents.

God, you open your hands and supply the real needs of every creature. We pray for your guidance and care that outdistance all our abilities to provide for ourselves. Give Tom and Joan work that will fulfill your purpose in their lives and help them provide food, shelter, clothing, and the beautiful things of life for their family. Steady their confidence when they are uncertain, and give them companionship when decisions have to be made.

Thank you, God, that Tom and Joan have been partners with each other and with you in creating and giving birth to a child. Grant them the grace to strengthen each other and Annette with love. May they continue to have access to each other's support through the power of your presence. May Tom and Joan relate to Annette with both strength and tenderness as they balance the power of love and insight.

Thank you, God, for the gift of life you have wrapped in Annette. She is yours. We have the privilege of knowing her and sharing life with her. In dedicating her to you, we dedicate ourselves because Tom and Joan and the church have knitted spirit to spirit with hers in the larger family of humankind. We pray that strength of personality and length of days may be hers to realize. Protect Annette from war, hunger, and rejection, but teach her the mystery of suffering.

Grant us your grace, mercy, and peace as we join Annette in her pilgrimage. We pray through Jesus Christ, the pioneer of our faith. Amen.

Baptism represents the dawning of faith in a person's life. It also is an opportune time for members of the congregation to reflect on the meaning of baptism for them as well as for the person being baptized. A prayer helps people focus on God's presence through baptism.

God,

As we participate with Greg in his baptism, we are reliving our own. We are thankful for this outward, visible expression that portrays what is occurring inwardly and invisibly. Thank you for Greg's faith in Jesus Christ as Savior and Sovereign. Thank you that Greg wants to be a part of the body of Christ. We celebrate the joy of Greg's salvation and ours. O God, we join our lives with his. His joys and sorrows become ours. May we do the work of Christ together compassionately and courageously.

God, guide Greg and us as we bury the past and rise to the present to love and serve you and one another. May Greg's baptism serve as a renewal of our commitment to be your ministers. In the name of the One who taught us to live by faith, we pray. Amen.

The one thing Christians have done every week for two thousand years is participate in communion. It is a comforting, troubling experience. Here is a prayer that expresses this:

Partaking of communion is troubling for us, God. To take the contents of this loaf and this cup into our bodies is to commit ourselves to pour out our lives in communicating your love for all people. Partaking together of communion says we all are part of the body of Christ. We are proclaiming more than we practice.

Help us, God, to renew our covenant with you now. As we partake of the elements, may we practice communion in our relationships, and may we daily grow toward being the body of Christ for you in our world. Amen.

A pivotal date for young people in our culture is the sixteenth birthday. It is valuable for the youth and the church to recognize this doorway that leads toward adulthood. Here is a litany of support for sixteen-year-olds:

Pastor: *We acknowledge that to become sixteen is a significant milestone in our culture.*

People: *We celebrate with these who have arrived at this threshold.*

Pastor: *To be sixteen is a key that unlocks many doors.*

People: *There is a mixture of freedom and responsibility behind those doors.*

Pastor: *We celebrate with you in this new freedom.*

People: *And we call you to meet the challenge of being a responsible person with your life—what you do with it, what you take into your life, and what comes out of your life.*

Pastor: *And we offer our prayers for you as the world opens before you.*

People: *We offer our support to undergird you as you launch out into the exciting unknown.*

Pastor: *May the love of God and our love bring you peace, encouragement, and support as you journey into a portion of life that has greater freedom and expanded responsibility.*

People: *Let it be so. Amen.*

For the congregations I have served as pastor, there have been annual services that held special meaning for people as they worshiped

God as a community of faith. Special times of worship have included Christmas Eve, Palm Sunday, Good Friday, and Easter. The following are prayers used in these services. This one is for Christmas Eve:

> Dear God,
>
> What a glorious, holy night this is! A night for kings and peasants, shepherds and angels, adults and children, wise people and fools—all their homage given to the newborn King.
>
> What a night! Even when our lives are in the shadows of despair, this night represents a glimmer of hope. Thank you, God, for breaking into our world.
>
> What a night! Even the Scrooges of the world have difficulty staying in character tonight. When you wrap your love in a human being, God, it's nearly impossible to resist!
>
> What a night! There are tensions and disturbances everywhere, yet there also are peace and calmness that go beyond our understanding. God, it's your peace, isn't it? It calls us to reshape our lives because there is a better way to live!
>
> What a night! Floods of joy fill our lives. How can we respond to you this night but with great joy?
>
> What a glorious, holy night this is, God! It is the brightest night of the year because we are more conscious of the Light of the world tonight than any other night. Thank you, God, for the Babe of Bethlehem who became the Man of Galilee to light the path of life for us. May we be the light of the world as Jesus said we are to be, and may our light begin shining tonight on this glorious, holy night. Amen.

The most contradictory day for worship for Christians is Palm Sunday. The day begins in joy but ends in despair. Expressing this struggle in prayer is helpful:

> God, this is a peculiar day at the beginning of an uncomfortable week. I wonder what went through Jesus' mind on this day twenty centuries ago. The mood was celebrative. The crowd was electric. Did Jesus think that people finally were understanding? Or was his

sudden popularity clear evidence to Jesus that the people had neither heard nor seen? What an emotional roller coaster Jesus must have ridden that week. To go from high acclaim to betrayal, denial, and death in five days is wrenching, blood-sweating agony.

God, I wonder if this day and this week are really any different from any other days and weeks. Do we not applaud your presence with loud hosannas every Sunday and then betray, deny, and crucify you before Friday has passed? O merciful God, forgive us. Forgive us for our piousness, hypocrisy, and religiosity. We make such a sham of your love. Forgive us.

O divine God, may our pilgrimage through this particular day and this uncomfortable week serve as both a mirror and a window so that we may see ourselves more honestly and see you more clearly. May our renewed vision enable us to follow you more nearly and serve you more dearly. Amen.

Good Friday is a religious oxymoron. The words identify a tragic day in history repeated often in our lives. Worship on this day is stark. The following litany expresses the mood:

Leader:	*We come together to remember the tragedy of Jesus' death,*
Congregation:	*And to mourn what we do when we have God in our hands.*
Leader:	*We remember Christ in the silence*
Congregation:	*Of the cross.*
Leader:	*We remember our brokenness*
Congregation:	*And the cross.*
Leader:	*We remember our loneliness*
Congregation:	*And the cross.*
Leader:	*We remember our commitment*
Congregation:	*And the cross.*
Leader:	*We come together to remember the tragedy of Jesus' death,*

Congregation: *And to mourn what we do when we have God in our hands.*

The great day of worship for Christians is Easter. It really is the first day of the year on the Christian calendar. Expressing through prayer something of the joy and celebration of the meaning of this day helps people open themselves to the resurrected living that God offers them.

O God, we are overwhelmed in the presence of your power. To restore life is something we are becoming able to do, but to resurrect one into continued living beyond this life is something only you have the power to do. Awareness of such power is awe-full for us.

God, we know that not only is resurrection a possibility for the future but it is also an existential reality now. But we cannot experience resurrection until we have confessed our sins to you. Numerous are our sins. Hear our confessions, O God, and deliver us from the death of sin to the resurrection of life. We have attempted to deal with our own sin through projection and repression. Deliver us, O God, through self-denial. In our close-mindedness we have refused to be teachable. Deliver us, O God, through humility. Too often we have yielded to the temptation of dealing only with ourselves and never getting beyond ourselves. Deliver us, O God, through sharing. How often we have functioned on the basis of superficial religion! Deliver us, O God, through understanding. We, too, have been the tragic figures of Judas and Peter. Deliver us, O God, through the abundant life you offer. Forgive us our sins and cleanse us from all unrighteousness.

All of us have gotten up out of sleep today, and in so doing we have experienced in a symbolic way what it means to rise to new life as we have come to experience and enjoy a new day. The sunlight and breezes of this day have given us a glimpse of what it means for you to dwell in our lives and to raise us from deadness. May this day be for our lives like a new moon rising, like the sun bursting forth on a frost-covered morning. O God, may every poetic and prosaic verse within our beings burst forth and communicate our love and joy for your calling us to rise and follow you.

Merciful God, comfort those in need today. The families of plane crash victims are overwhelmed by grief. Ease their sorrow. Those whose homes were washed away by floodwaters are stunned by their losses. Soothe their pain. The leaders of countries great and small have the destinies of the world's people in their hands. Steady their decisions that they might be reasonable, peaceful, and understanding. Our community has made strides in human relationships, but we have miles to go before we sleep. Guide us in leavening our community with your love and justice.

Now, God, we are eager and ready to renew our covenant with you. Come to us now, and resurrect us from our deadness into sensitive, alive persons. We offer our prayer in the name of the Resurrection and the Life. Amen.

Worship is prayer, and prayer is worship. Private praying helps prepare us to join in worship with a community of faith. Prayers in public worship help us examine who we are and rehearse who God is calling us to be.

QUESTIONS TO PONDER

1. How are prayers in public worship rehearsal for you?
2. What causes a prayer offered by another to become your prayer?
3. Pretend that you are the worship leader for the congregation where you worship. Write the prayers for a worship service.
4. What did you discover about yourself in writing the prayers suggested in the previous question? How did you experience God in this process?
5. What do you think George Buttrick might have meant by his statement to "get the prayers right" for public worship?

CHAPTER TWELVE

A World of Praying to Do

LUKE 4:16–19

We cannot pray for very long before the circle of inclusion moves beyond ourselves, our families, our friends, to embrace acquaintances, colleagues, neighbors, people we do not know and will never meet. Indeed, there is a world to be prayed for and a world of praying to do. Praying like Jesus leads us to pray for the world because the circle of concern and prayer that Jesus drew encompassed the globe.

Every person has a worldview. It may be limited and provincial or expansive and cosmopolitan. Whatever a person's worldview, the good news of Christ pushes the boundaries of the world and challenges people to be inclusive. This good news pushed on Peter's worldview until he discovered that nothing God had created was unclean, including the Gentile Cornelius. Paul, after being confronted by this good news and wrestling with its implications, made the revolutionary statement that there is neither Jew nor Greek, neither slave nor free, neither male nor female, but that all are one in Christ Jesus. A person's worldview affects how that person prays for the world. As people pray for the world, their worldview is affected.

Many factors influence and impact our lives. These factors affect why, how, when, and for what we pray. William Sloane Coffin offered this opinion: "A liberal is a person who thinks other people need help, and a radical is one who knows we're all in trouble."[1] This kind of radicality causes many to see the need to pray for the world. My world consciousness is continually being raised through the events that transpire in news stories. Living in an international community puts human faces on racism, hunger, and poverty. I become increasingly aware that this is one world under one God, and what happens to one person affects all persons. Martin Luther King Jr. said it more profoundly: "All life is inter-related. We are all caught in an inescapable network of mutuality, tied into a single garment of destiny. Whatever affects one directly, affects all indirectly. We are made to live together because of the inter-related structure of reality."[2]

The solidarity of the human condition causes me to empathize with people who are poor, captives, blind, and oppressed. Consciousness-raising causes me to realize that I really do not comprehend the impact that poverty, hunger, unemployment, imprisonment, and war have on the lives of people. Only as I have looked into the eyes of a few of these people have I seen the hollowness, the desperation, and the deep yearning for help that cause me to cry out with them and for them. Prayer puts us in touch with people with needs, concerns, values, dreams, and pains. Bonding occurs as we share our commonality in prayer.

I attended a press conference held by diverse religious leaders in support of prayer but in opposition to a proposed constitutional amendment. A female rabbi, a Jewish girl, a Buddhist monk, a Piscataway Indian, a Black Muslim, and a Christian minister offered prayers to God. A breadth of ideologies and views was represented, but regardless of name, all were addressing God. Each prayer invited God's help for the one praying to be sensitive to others and to protect one from imposing one's views or convictions on others. I had a keen sense of the presence of God and of solidarity with these people. We were at one with one another and with God. This is a microcosm of the world and what the world needs.

Surely, one thing we can do is to pray for the world. When we pray for the world, a bonding with the hurt and the hungry, the terrified and the terrorists, the helpless and the hopeless occurs. Neither they nor we can remain the same as we pray for them. The barriers begin to come down, and we discover ourselves crossing lines we never thought we would cross.

The following prayer illustrates how prayer may begin with personal awareness and often pivot as the one praying is turned from an inward, narrow vision to an outward, expanding view of the needs of the world:

Grand and Glorious Creator,

The weeks of autumn have enabled us to behold the beauty of the earth. Such beauty has caused us to contemplate your beauty behind and beyond earthly beauty. In recent days, we have had a glimpse of Saturn and paused to worship you, the Master Designer of this solar system and others. Just this morning, as we arose from the death we call sleep, we were awed by the function of our bodies and concluded that we are wonderfully made. Such discovery has caused us to search for the depth of our existence. We have discovered that our lives are gifts from you. We are your handiwork. Thus, the basis of our genuine gratitude is the awareness and confession that we are created in your image.

O Maker of us all, we are wonderfully made. We thank you for good minds that help us grasp knowledge and find truth. We are grateful for free will that allows us to choose our own direction and enables us to discover that we are not ourselves apart from you. Thank you, God, for imagination that enables us to dream and picture ideals. We are grateful for personality that causes us to flesh out our dreams and ideals.

Keep us ever mindful that we are yours, that this is one world you have made, and that we are partners together as your servants to bring health and healing to your world and to your people. May the causes for which we campaign be permeated with love, justice, and mercy. May we be committed to the priority of an integrated community—integrated culturally, socially, economically, religiously, and racially. May our corner of the world reflect the harmony, diversity, and unity that you dream for all your worlds. May the bonds that unify us always be stronger than the differences that threaten to divide us.

We thank you, dear God, for your unmerited favor so generously showered upon us. May the authenticity for our thanksgiving be demonstrated through thanksliving. Amen.

There is a sense in which prayer, whether private or public, when it gets beyond rote memory and empty phrases, begins to thaw our loyalties. This is evident in the racist who cannot be cruel to the African American child living next door or the greedy person disturbed to action by the starving face of a street person she could not get past quickly enough. When God wraps the needs of the world in human flesh, it is difficult to resist. Once a person starts praying for these people and their needs, the resistance is reduced even more.

Here is a prayer that refers to two people who made significant contributions to tear down the dividing wall of racial prejudice in their community. Expressing gratitude to God for their contributions caused me to pray for righteousness, mercy, and justice in the community.

Lover of us all, accept our gratitude for your gifts of life and love. Thank you for calling us into partnership with you and with one another that we might collaborate in bringing your universe to fulfillment and completion.

God, thank you for the contributions that Councilman Fischer and Chief Reeves have made toward the betterment of humankind. Continue to encourage them and us in our endeavors to make the communities where we live oases of openness and acceptance in the deserts of antagonism and hatred.

Regardless of the strides that have been made in human relationships, God, we know we have missed the mark of your intentions for us. We confess that we have hugged our prejudices and have locked ourselves behind doors of fear. We confess that as long as justice is realized for us, we have little concern about justice for all. Much of our work for justice for all has been tempered more with prejudice against those who are prejudiced than being tempered with mercy and kindness and righteousness for all.

But you, O God, want all of us to do justice, to love kindness, and to walk humbly with you. You are the drummer setting the cadence for our marching, and the cadence calls for justice to roll down like water and righteousness like an ever-flowing stream. No one is to be omitted in being treated justly and rightly. That is given in your gracious creativity in making us in your image.

May we with renewed sensitivity and expanded vigor increase our sphere of influence for justice and righteousness. May we evaluate this day and every day of living by asking ourselves if we have done justice, loved kindness, and walked humbly with you. These are the beats of a different drummer for some of us, but now more than ever we need to march to your cadence and make your cadence our own. May it be so in my life and in every life. Amen.

The problems and threats in the world are enormous. We are inundated with facts and figures about ecology and people who are hungry, poor, unemployed, and diseased. Our skills seem to match few of the needs. If they do, they wouldn't make a dent in the problems. We become immobilized. We struggle to find a place to begin, and thus, we do not start. The old Chinese proverb states that the journey of a thousand miles begins with a single step.

With regard to the magnitude of the needs of the world, what is the first step? Prayer is a first step. This is a simple but not a simplistic response. Prayer is an active, engaging, encountering dialogue with God. We must learn to pray for the specific needs of the world. William Sloane Coffin complains, "There is too much dignity in too many prayers—dignity at the expense of specificity. . . . So never mind how crude or how trivial your prayers may sound. There are no unimportant tears to God."[3]

My first awareness of world hunger came via television when I saw the pictures from Bangladesh of starving children with bloated stomachs. I was stunned and immobilized by what I saw. My first prayers for the hungry had no words. Actually, I did not even recognize them as prayers at the time. Those pictures would not let me go, and I wonder now if it were love that would not let me go. My first verbal prayer response was, "This problem is so enormous. What can I do that would make a difference?" Of course, this rhetorical question in prayer was intended to be answered with "nothing" and free me to go on to problems that I could solve. I was content with my "nothing" answer. Perhaps the Spirit of God continued to intercede for me, nudging me to open my eyes, my ears, and my life to the needs of hungry people. My prayer had the same words but with a different emphasis: "What can *I* do that would make a difference?"

I have become more open to articles about hunger that inform me about the problem of and possible solutions to hunger. I now get more regular exercise and eat less than at any time in my life, and this is a direct result of my awareness of people who are hungry. Starving millions and weight-watching millions exist in this global village. Prayer is a place for us to begin concerning people who are hungry, praying for them, and praying that we might be part of the solution. When praying for those who are hungry, ask, "What can I do that will make a difference?" Such a prayer puts us in touch with those who are hungry. Once God gets us out of isolation, the possibilities are multiple. Here is a prayer about excess that may raise our consciousness:

O God,

Often we are warmed by being identified as the light and salt of the earth. But the warmth turns icy cold when in honesty we become conscious of how far short we are of being who and what you have invited us to be.

We have lived excessively. We eat too much, we drink too much, and we work too much. Through our excesses, we have sinned against you, against others, and against ourselves. We have harmed our lives, your gifts to us. Forgive us. We have taken food from others by overconsuming it for ourselves. We suffer from unlimited wanting and equate wants with needs. Forgive us. At least once a year we open our eyes to those who do not have enough. God, help us to do something about empty stomachs in January and July as well as in November. We have too much while others have too little. May we be part of the solution to this problem, and may we begin now. Amen.

Jesus said that foxes have holes and birds have nests, but the Human One had nowhere to lay his head. I don't comprehend the impact of that statement because I always have had a place to go. Never have I been homeless. I see homeless people, and I shudder in realizing that the street is home for them. Everything they own—consisting of the clothes they wear—is in plain view. Only a piece of newspaper is between them and the bitter winter cold. Sometime during the day they may make it to a soup kitchen for enough food to keep them existing for another day. At best, these street people are existing. I am shocked at what life is for them.

How we relate to other people, especially when they are in need, is the acid test of how we relate to Christ. I have lots of company in my discomfort with homeless people and my desire to avoid them and to pretend I do not see them. There is no lasting comfort in knowing I have partners in my discomfort and in my detached approach to human need.

I seem compelled to pray for people who are homeless. Once again my loyalties thaw a little as a result, and I begin identifying with them. This is a start toward reaching out to them.

God,

I don't want to admit that John is a human being. I justify my distance if he is a statistic, just one of the millions who are homeless and helpless.

What happened to John? He is out of work, and no wonder. He is unclean and unkempt. Who would hire him? He doesn't want to work or he'd get a job. The paper is full of want ads every day. I can keep my smugness as long as John stays downtown, and I stay in sanitary suburbia. But, God, once I walk on John's street and look into his eyes, he won't go away. Those empty, hollow, haggard eyes won't leave me alone.

What happened to John? When he came as a child, we turned him away. He always sat in the back of the class at school, just on the fringe. He wasn't sure anyone would accept him, and we didn't. He was slow with the answers, and so the teacher gave her attention to the quick children. We did, too, because we needed her approval to survive. We kept pushing John to the edge. When the jobs came, we ran past John, took the good ones for ourselves, and told John he could have what was left. Once we had him on the edge, we wanted to keep him there. We spat on him with ridicule and kicked him with contempt. We middle-of-the-roaders need marginal people like John to help us be sure we are in the middle and not on the edge. Now John is about to fall off the edge. He is grasping for any morsel that we might drop.

O God, look at what we've done to your son. We're crucifying another one of your children. John condemns us. No, we have condemned ourselves. We see our condemnation in his eyes. That is where we hear you say, "It is I." God, forgive us! John's eyes have condemned us, and they have awakened us. Help us to go to the edge and pull John and Mary and Tom back into life. Amen.

Nearly any town or city I visit I see people begging. This is not a new phenomenon. Jesus said we would always have the poor with us, which is an indictment of us rather than a commentary about people who are poor. Sometimes I see beggars standing at busy intersections with signs around their necks. Other times they are in busy pedestrian areas. Often they are women with small children. Occasionally, they are physically disabled. Always they look and sound needy. Recently, I allowed myself to become engaged emotionally, and I saw a beggar differently. I uttered this prayer as a result:

She caught my eye, God. I was sitting nearby and seemed unable to take my eyes off her. Her bronze, smooth face depicted youth. Her dark, clear eyes were magnetic. Her clothing showed the wear of several days. The nine-month-old child in her lap was docile. She sat at the gate of the Old City and begged for alms as people have done for centuries.

The reactions in my head ran the gamut, God. Surely, she is in need, or she would not be sitting here with her child like this all day, day after day. I had seen her other days as I passed by. But today I was sitting and watching. As I watched, I watched her work. Her eyes were keen as to when people were coming. She timed their approach and spoke to them with outstretched hand as they were three or four steps away. Her voice was loud enough to catch attention but soft enough to make words difficult to distinguish. Passersby adjusted their stride a bit and looked in her direction. One out of ten stopped to give her a coin or two—one shekel, five shekels, maybe ten. Quickly, she put the coins in the pocket of her blouse so that her hand was empty when the next person came by.

Those who gave her something were as varied as the people who passed by. A mother with a young child stopped. It took her some time to fish a coin out of her purse, but she was determined to give to this woman with a child. An early retiree gave as he continued moving. A black man passed by and fifteen paces later, stopped, did a U-turn, and gave her two coins. Some never let her catch their gaze. That was their defense or their disgust or both.

God, I'm sure people gave for different reasons. Some gave because they perceived a need. Some gave because they felt pity for this woman or maybe more so for her little boy. He played for a while with an empty film box and then for a moment with a cellophane candy wrapper. He became fussy and she became irritated.

Two or three vendors conversed with her. To one man she gave a handful of coins. Who was he? Was this her job? What was happening here, God?

Like all of us, this woman had needs, but what were they? Was this her gainful employment? Hardly what any of us would consider a meaningful job! Was this all an act and the tiny child one of the props? She appeared to be a professional. Was she or had she done this so long that she had developed the "art of begging"? God, don't let my cynicism rule me. Was this woman desperate? Had she tried everything she knew to do to provide for her child, and begging was her last resort? Was the way I treated her the way I treat you, God?

This is a troubling picture, God. How can your mercy touch all of us who are in the picture—the beggar, the child, the givers, the passersby, and the spectators? God, please touch her, touch her baby, touch me. Heal our lives and make us whole people. Hear my prayer, O God, our Redeemer. Amen.

The literature of civilization is filled with compositions expressing longings for peace. Micah (4:1–7) and other biblical writers expressed what peace is. The biblical understanding of peace means the state of wholeness possessed by persons or groups. The characteristics of this wholeness include health, prosperity, and security as a result of spiritual completeness of the covenant relationship with God. There is no greater longing in Scripture than the longing for world peace. How much more intense this yearning is for many today. When the atomic bomb was developed, we moved into the nuclear age, and nothing has been so constant as the turbulent change that has occurred since 1945. The lack of wholeness runs the gamut of needs in my city. On one end of the spectrum are those who are homeless and those who have no idea when or if they will eat again. On the other end are those who have plenty to eat but who are gravely concerned about the annihilation of the entire human race.

Maybe in no arena do we feel more helpless than in working for world peace. We suffer from what Robert Jay Lifton calls "psychic numbing."[4] Yet no one predicted how many voices would begin to be raised against nuclear armaments. No one imagined that 500,000 demonstrators would gather at the United Nations in June 1982 in a peaceful peace demonstration. Where did this movement begin? It bubbled up in the church, and now is flowing out into the world. It began with people praying for the world and for themselves. We can pray for peace in our relationships, and we can offer our energies to be used for peace throughout the world.

O God, our Creator, we are partners with you in creating the world as we know it today. Never has your title, Creator, brought such condemnation upon us as it now does. We are the crown of your creation. We are your handiwork, which you announced was "very good." What manner of evil has brought us to the point where we can not only wipe out all of creation but also end the human enterprise altogether? We know that such power is demonic because we have no authority to use this destructive power. O God, forgive us for the demon that we have created.

O God, our Savior, we are demon possessed by our clamor for security. We are permitting our fears to control us. We need to be depossessed. We know that authentic security rests with you and that your love casts out fear. Help us to trust you rather than ourselves and to allow your love to wash away our fears. Help us to defuse our bombs and direct our energy and resources away from destructiveness and divisiveness toward human wholeness. God, make us look into the faces of those we would destroy. Help us to see that we have made them our shadow sides. Make us know that to destroy them is to destroy ourselves. Convince us that they are your children too. They have families and friends just as we do. They have dreams and ambitions just as we do. They have needs and hurts just as we do. They need us, and we need them. God, protect us from destroying one another.

O God, our Sustainer, help us to be partners with you in sustaining the world. We are family, your family. Making peace begins with me, doesn't it, God? It begins with how I relate to those in my primary relationships. Help me to sow the seeds of peace rather than violence with my family and friends. Help me to develop these gifts of peacemaking: affirmation of others, respect for the differences of others, the challenge of cooperation, and creative resolution of conflict. God, improve my peacemaking efforts at home. Sustain peace in your world by beginning with me.

O God, our Redeemer, instruct us in redemptive ways to resolve conflict. Enable us to love our enemies and to pray for those who persecute us. Forgive us for our desires and plans to destroy others. Permeate our lives with an attitude of forgiveness. Enable us to forgive without limit because we have been forgiven without limit. Guide us to create peace where there is hatred and reconciliation where there is separation.

Dear God, make us instruments of your peace. May our partnership with you as Creator, Sustainer, and Redeemer cause us to beat our destructive attitudes into constructive relationships. May we be makers of peace where we live and work and play. May your peace permeate the world, and may it begin with me today. Amen.

As our sensitivity to others increases, we become more aware of the wars that are raging in people's lives. Unless they find some peace in their lives, they will project their rage onto others. In one sense, people always are living in troubled times. Here is a prayer for peace for people living in such unrest:

God,

We are living in troubled times. Our lives are but brief interludes between birth and death, and these interludes are filled with pain and suffering. There seems to be no ease for us; there is no balm in Gilead for us. We hear proclamations of peace on earth, goodwill to people, but there are times when it seems there is no peace because hate is strong and mocks the song of peace on earth, goodwill to people.

God, I feel so for the Palestinians. The oppression they are experiencing is heavy. The pressure builds as they see and feel the unfairness. The pressure boils and for some spills over into violent acts. How can it not? How many cheeks can they turn, God? Violent reactions are understandable but not acceptable. Many Palestinians have seen a better way. They are seeking to respond nonviolently. They are striving to work for peace with justice.

What a day that will be! What an example of lion and lamb lying down together when Palestinians and Israelis live together in peace, when the cages are removed, the borders are opened, and both

Palestinians and Israelis are free! God, make it happen now! Until peace comes, may tolerance abound so they do not destroy one another, but learn to respect one another. As long as there is no peace for them, there is no peace for us. They are our brothers and sisters in your family, God. When any part of your family is in trouble, all of us are in trouble. Help them and us study and learn to live in peace with one another. May justice flow like a never-ending stream, and may all of our voices raise in joyful antiphony shouting, "Peace on earth to all people of good will." Amen.

One of the greatest needs is for peace and justice to permeate our living. As they take root in our lives, we will not only pray for peace and justice but also practice them. Here is a prayer expressing the desire for peace and justice:

Every age has been the best of times and the worst of times, God. We have more with which to cope—more tension, more broken relationships. We also have more resources—better technology, better medical attention, more freedom to find solutions.

God, we know there are many near us who are not at peace. We see their unrest and feel their discomfort. Grant that we might be peacemakers in their lives and be a part of the solution to the tension that is destroying them. Come in peace for them through us. Just when we think life is in order for us, a crisis arises that disrupts our plans and intentions. Help us to know that you are seeking to come in peace to us today. Enable us to be receptive to your coming. We offer our prayer in the name of the ultimate peacemaker, Jesus Christ, our Sovereign. Amen.

Then there was the man I met in the refugee camp in Bethlehem. What irony that there still is no room in that city! I listened to his story and heard the rage that has been building for fifty years. Is it any wonder that area is like a tinderbox? I was disturbed by his story. I took my disturbance to God:

God,

Abraham Sheheim is one of your unique creations. Traveling the curves and lines of his face is the record of his story, his life. The sparkle in his eyes still displays the energy and enthusiasm of youth, but the crow's-feet that surround them disclose a difficult journey that still has many unanswered questions.

The pain and heartbreak began when he was sixteen. That was when the soldiers came charging into his village. He and his family were told they would have to leave but would be able to return to their home in ten days, twelve at the most. That was fifty years ago. He still holds the keys to his house, although the house is no longer standing. It has long since been bulldozed to the ground and another built in its place on his family's property.

O God, I cannot imagine what it was like at the tender age of sixteen, as the oldest child in his family, for Abraham to be thrust into the role of taking care of his mother and his younger brothers and sisters. The only place for them to go was to the refugee camp near Hebron. Then they spent the winter at a camp in Jericho, and after the winter came to the camp near Bethlehem where he has been until this day.

Abraham comments immediately that he has been luckier than most. He has been able to find jobs outside the camp at various times that enabled him to semi-provide for his family. Why hasn't he done something else? Why hasn't he left the camp for good? He is trapped. If he leaves the camp permanently, he forfeits his right to claim the land in his home village that belonged to his family. Where would he go, and what would he do? He doesn't have the means to purchase land, and even if he had the means, he would not be permitted because he is a Palestinian living in the state of Israel. What a dilemma!

Abraham rails at the Israelis for their mistreatment. He rails at the United States for being a partner in establishing the state of Israel and disenfranchising the Palestinians. He rails at the unfairness of losing his home, his land, his village, and his community. And why shouldn't he?

O God, can't you do something? Won't you do something? Can I do something? Please help the Israelis and Palestinians learn to trust one another and live in peace so that Abraham can finish his days in peace. May the lines in his face run to a happy ending. Help me, help all of us, to be part of the solution. In the name of the One who came in peace and who brings peace beyond our understanding, Amen.

Prayer puts us in touch with other people. As we pray for specific persons and about definite world situations, we begin to develop a bond with those people and their conditions. If we are serious about intercessory prayer, then is not part of our reason for praying to place part of our energy at God's disposal to use as God is able for those persons and their conditions? Praying for the world includes the troubles and conflicts that other nations experience.

O Divine One,

Ours is a troubled generation living in a disturbed world. Trouble occurs in many places in the world. There are wars and threats of war. There are injustice and unfair distribution of wealth. There are oppressors and oppressed.

There is trouble in the Middle East. I'm grateful for any cease-fire, no matter how temporary it seems to be. Always I hope this temporary agreement will become a permanent one. May the Arabs, Palestinians, and Jews discover that they are more alike than different, and may they work for their mutual benefit.

Wholesale murders happen too often by governments, gangs, and drive-by shootings. These tragedies are revolting to us. We do not understand. God, help the victims and their families, and help those who murdered. We cannot excuse their deeds, but we sense their terror and helplessness. Calm them, God.

God, bring peace to Ireland. I wonder how many people have prayed for that and how many more have worked for peace there. Christians have more in common than our conflicts, but we cannot prove that in Ireland. God, I ache deep in my soul when I hear and see the bitterness and animosity hurled between Protestants and Catholics there. God, may their constructive efforts toward the brotherhood and sisterhood of humanity bear fruit.

God, we feel there is trouble on every hand. Reassure us that we are not without a Friend. Protect us from despair that could easily beset us. Make us to see that all is not lost, and challenge us to be at peace with all people, beginning with our families and friends whom we see daily. We offer our prayer like Jesus, the Maker of peace who teaches us to be makers of peace. Amen.

The direction of nations and the destinies of people are determined by the decisions of national lawmakers and leaders. Decision makers vary from democratic to autocratic to totalitarian. Many of us have no concept of the pressures these persons feel or the strain under which many of them work. Some of them at times are unaware of how heavy their task weighs upon their lives.

We need to pray for world decision makers because their loads are heavy, as are ours, because they are limited human beings, as are we, because we need to better understand them, and because we are partners with them as managers of the world. Our prayers for them are not to baptize their actions but to guide them and us toward clearer thinking in making decisions that will benefit all people everywhere.

O God,

Many people will make decisions today that will affect our lives. They are power brokers in nations great and small, and they hold the destinies of the world's people in their hands. Steady their decisions so that they might be reasonable, peaceful, and understanding. We have made strides in human relationships, but we have miles to go before we sleep. Guide all of us who make decisions to leaven the world with love and justice.

Thank you, God, for persons throughout the world who are willing to be decision makers. We appreciate their willingness to be decision makers. We appreciate their willingness to expose themselves to the public eye and public scrutiny. The issues with which they must deal are mind-boggling. Protect them from being overwhelmed by their nations' agendas, and grant them the wisdom to deal sanely with the issues one at a time. Give them needed patience to work equitable compromises that will help meet the needs of people, and offer them the necessary strength to struggle to find the best solutions for all people. Prevent them from giving in to the pressures of special interest groups, and do not let the serpent of personal advancement blind their wisdom and insight.

God, we are grateful for the energy and enthusiasm that you generate in world decision makers to enable them to deal with tough issues. Do not permit them to become so power hungry that they fail to care for the hungry; do not let them bask in the warmth of popularity so long that they forget those who are cold and unpopular; do not let them become so enamored with their positions that they are out of touch with those who have no position; do not let them be seduced by might-makes-right schemes that always reduce people to pawns on a political chessboard.

As these decision makers go about their daily tasks, make them mindful of your presence and of your desire to be a partner with them in their decisions. May your love undergird them, may your joy hover over them, may your hope go before them, and may your peace permeate their lives and their relationships. Thank you for hearing our prayer and attending to our concerns. Amen.

As our worldview enlarges, the global village shrinks. With instant news we are bombarded by events of destruction, violence, terrorism, and suffering. Overwhelmed by such events, we feel threatened, insecure, and vulnerable. We want to withdraw and come out only when absolutely necessary—to go to work and to get supplies. A common protective maneuver is to isolate. We need to pray for the lonely people of the world as a start toward building community.

God, we are lonely people.
We are lonely because of the losses we have experienced, because of choices we have made, because of what has been done to us, because of what we have done.

God, we are all lovely people.
We are lovely because you have made us and because you love us.
We need fellowship that is more than eating.
We need caring that is more than empty phrases.
We need to look at one another and see love looking back at us.
We need bridges of loveliness to cross over our loneliness. Amen.

If people struggle as much in their attempts to pray for the world as I have struggled in attempting to write about praying for the world, then no wonder the world is in the condition it is. E. B. White has delineated clearly the issue for me: "If the world were merely seductive, that would be easy. If it were merely challenging that would be no problem, but I arise in the morning torn between a desire to improve (or save) the world and a desire to enjoy (or savor) the world. This makes it hard to plan the day."[5]

One who has been above the world expresses what our perspective of the world needs to be. Joseph Allen was one of the astronauts on the last precommercial flight of the space shuttle *Columbia.* He said that from space, as one looks at the earth, there are no distinctions of people by color, race, or social, economic, or philosophical persuasion. It is all one entity.

Maybe none of us ever will have the opportunity to view the world from outer space, but if we seek to pray like Jesus, we will discover that the view of the world both from outer space and from inner space is the same. There are no distinctions of people. The world is all one entity.

Praying is an evolving process. It is a direction rather than a station. My prayer learning has been telescopic in nature. Being most conscious of my needs and inadequacies, I usually begin praying for myself; however, I cannot pray long before I become conscious of the needs of others, and praying begins to have social dimensions. "I" becomes "we" and "my" becomes "our." I hope you will join me in this lifelong pilgrimage of praying like Jesus because there is a world of praying to do.

QUESTIONS TO PONDER

1. What do you consider the most difficult part about praying for the world?
2. What happens to you when you pray for the world?
3. Does praying for the world make the world seem larger or smaller to you? Why?
4. Why do you think you should pray for the world?
5. When you pray for the world, are there some things you seem always to be praying for? What are they?

Notes

INTRODUCTION

1. Charles Britt, "A Letter of Opinion," *Lee County Eagle,* June 1, 1997, A3.

1. JESUS AGONIZED

1. Gerhard Kittel, *Theological Dictionary of the New Testament,* vol. 5 (Grand Rapids, Mich.: Eerdmans, 1964), 984–85.
2. Will Campbell, *God on Earth* (New York: Crossroad, 1983), 6.
3. Quoted by Henri Nouwen in "Who Will Mourn? Who Will Dance?" (Notre Dame, Ind.: Ave Maria Press, Modern Cassette Library, 1996).
4. Sister Gillian Leslie, O.D.C., "Acceptance of His Father's Will," *Living Pulpit* 3, no. 1 (1994): 41.
5. Nouwen, "Who Will Mourn? Who Will Dance?"

2. JESUS PRAYED HIS LIFE

1. Glenn Hinson, *A Serious Call to a Contemplative Lifestyle* (Philadelphia: Westminster Press, 1974), 71.
2. Glenn Hinson, *The Reaffirmation of Prayer* (Nashville: Broadman Press, 1979), 31.
3. Nick Davis, "An Interview with Ken Medema, Part 2," *Baptists Today* 12, no. 22 (November 1994).
4. Quoted from Midrash Berakoth VI by Lamar Williamson Jr., in *Interpretation: A Bible Commentary for Teaching and Preaching, Mark* (Louisville: John Knox Press, 1983), 253.
5. William Barclay, *The Daily Study Bible,* vol. 2 (Philadelphia: Westminster Press, 1958), 331.

3. WHO AM I?

1. Albrecht Oepke, "Baptizo," in *Theological Dictionary of the New Testament,* ed. Gerhard Kittel and Gerhard Friedrich, vol. 1 (Grand Rapids, Mich.: Eerdmans, 1964), 530.

2. William Barclay, *The Mind of Jesus* (New York: Harper and Brothers, 1960), 19.

3. Ibid., 22.

4. WHAT AM I TO DO?

1. Werner Foerster, "Diabolos," in *Theological Dictionary of the New Testament,* ed. Gerhard Kittel and Gerhard Friedrich, vol. 2 (Grand Rapids, Mich.: Eerdmans, 1964), 72–81

2. M. Scott Peck, *People of the Lie: The Hope for Healing Human Evil* (New York: Simon & Schuster, 1983), 206.

3. John R. Claypool, "The Power Problem," sermon given at Broadway Baptist Church, Fort Worth, Texas, July 14, 1973.

5. THE LEARNER'S PRAYER

1. Elton Trueblood, *The Lord's Prayers* (New York: Harper & Row, 1965), 26.

2. Bruce Chilton, *Jesus' Prayer and Jesus' Eucharist: His Personal Practice of Spirituality* (Valley Forge, Pa.: Trinity Press International, 1997), 27.

3. Patrick D. Miller, *They Cried to the Lord* (Minneapolis: Fortress Press, 1994), 329.

4. Campbell, *God on Earth,* 17.

5. Chilton, *Jesus' Prayer and Jesus' Eucharist,* 48.

6. Sidney Lanier, "The Marshes of Glynn," in *Poems and Letters* (Baltimore: Johns Hopkins University Press, 1945), 48.

7. Chilton, *Jesus' Prayer and Jesus' Eucharist,* 43–44.

6. GOD, PROTECT THEM FROM EVIL

1. Chilton, *Jesus' Prayer and Jesus' Eucharist,* 73, 75.

2. Ibid., 56.

3. William Hull, "John," in *The Broadman Bible Commentary,* vol. 9 (Nashville: Broadman Press, 1970), 346.

7. JESUS' LAST WISH AND TESTAMENT

1. Kurt Aland et al., eds., *The Greek New Testament* (London: United Bible Society, 1966), 311.

2. Carlyle Marney, *He Became Like Us* (Nashville: Abingdon Press, 1964), 18.

3. Arthur John Gossip, "John," in *The Interpreter's Bible,* vol. 8 (Nashville: Abingdon Press, 1952), 782.

4. Henry Turlington, "Mark," in *The Broadman Bible Commentary,* vol. 8 (Nashville: Broadman Press, 1969), 397.

5. From a sermon I heard George Buttrick deliver in the chapel at the Southern Baptist Theological Seminary, Louisville, Ky., spring 1973.

6. Frank Stagg, "Matthew," in *The Broadman Bible Commentary,* vol. 8, 246.

7. Gossip, "John," 785.

8. PRAYING FOR YOURSELF

1. Sarah Ban Breathnach, *Simple Abundance: A Daybook of Comfort and Joy* (New York: Warner Books, 1995), November 8 entry.

9. PRAYING FOR FRIENDS AND ENEMIES

1. Paul E. Johnson, *Psychology of Religion* (New York: Abingdon Press, 1959), 132.

2. David Elkind, "The Child's Conception of Prayer," in *The Child's Reality: Three Developmental Themes* (Hillsdale, N.J.: Laurence Erlbaum Associates, 1978), 27–45.

3. Donald Capps, "The Psychology of Petitionary Prayer," *Theology Today* 32, no. 2 (1982): 130.

4. Theodore Newcomb, "An Approach to the Study of Communication," *Psychological Review* 60 (1953): 392–403.

10. GRIEF PRAYING

1. Ned Cassem, psychiatrist at Harvard University, from a lecture given at Johns Hopkins Hospital, April 1979.

2. Granger Westberg, *Good Grief* (Philadelphia: Fortress Press, 1962).

11. PRAYING IS WORSHIP

1. George Buttrick, class lecture, Louisville Presbyterian Seminary, Louisville, Kentucky, spring 1972.

12. A WORLD OF PRAYING TO DO

1. William Sloane Coffin, American Baptist Peace Conference, Washington, D.C., November 11, 1982.

2. Martin Luther King Jr., quoted by Maynard Shelly, *New Call for Peacemakers* (Newton, Kans.: Faith & Life Press, 1979), 12.

3. William Sloane Coffin, *The Courage to Love* (New York: Harper & Row, 1982), 25.

4. David M. Alpern, "Who's Who in the Movement," *Newsweek,* April 26, 1982, 22–23.

5. E. B. White, *International Herald Tribune,* July 13, 1968, 16.